Bringing Classes into
the Public Library

Bringing Classes into the Public Library

A Handbook for Librarians

MARTHA SEIF SIMPSON
AND LUCRETIA I. DUWEL

McFarland & Company, Inc., Publishers
Jefferson, North Carolina, and London

Martha Seif Simpson has also written these
works for McFarland: *Reading Programs for Young Adults* (1997);
Environmental Awareness Activities for Librarians and Teachers (1995);
and *Summer Reading Clubs* (1992); and with coauthor Lynne Perrigo
StoryCraft: 50 Theme-Based Programs (2001)

Illustrations by Mark A. Hatfield

LIBRARY OF CONGRESS CATALOGUING-IN-PUBLICATION DATA

Simpson, Martha Seif, 1954–
Bring classes into the public library :
a handbook for librarians /
Martha Seif Simpson and Lucretia I. Duwel.
p.   cm.
Includes index.

ISBN-13: 978-0-7864-2806-9
(softcover : 50# alkaline paper) ∞

1. Libraries and students—United States.
2. Libraries and schools—United States.
3. Children's libraries—Marketing—Handbooks, manuals, etc.
I. Duwel, Lucretia I., 1948–   II. Title.
Z718.7S48 2007   027.62'5—dc22   2006037527

British Library cataloguing data are available

Cover photograph ©2007 Photodisc

Manufactured in the United States of America

*McFarland & Company, Inc., Publishers
Box 611, Jefferson, North Carolina 28640
www.mcfarlandpub.com*

To all our colleagues past and present
in the Stratford Library and the Stratford schools
who initiated, developed and supported this program
for all of the youth of Stratford

Table of Contents

Introduction

There is a great opportunity right now in public libraries for Youth Services librarians to work with schools. If our goal is to provide the best possible service to our student patrons, then collaboration with the schools is mandatory. As public librarians, we understand this after more than two decades of partnering with school media specialists and teachers. The realization that we serve the same children and teens led to our recently adopted phrase: "The schools have them from 8 to 2 and the public librarians have them from 2 to 8!" This simple mantra epitomizes the essence of this book.

The commitment for a program of class visits at your library could begin as a discussion with a single teacher, a directive from school or library administrators, or even from the ideas presented in this book. It is our intent to present a framework that has been successful for us along with variations and situations that we have experienced or envisioned. It is meant to be a workbook and a work in progress. It is a nuts-and-bolts approach to get you started by describing in detail how a structured series of class visits across a grade level can be accomplished. Chapters address procedures, planning, and implementation of class visits. Also included are discussions of possible challenges, workable solutions, and an analysis of the outcomes and impact of the program. The appendices contain reproducible documents such as sample schedules, letters to teachers, evaluation forms, several types of student activity sheets, and other templates to enable you to begin your own program of class visits once you have made the decision to provide this important service.

Currently, many public libraries do allow for occasional or individual class visits, which are usually set up at the request of a teacher. Your library may already have one or more "class visit programs"—that is, regular presentations that you do whenever a teacher calls to arrange a field trip to the public library. But this hit-or-miss approach does not guarantee that other classes of that grade level will follow suit, nor is it any assurance that the same teacher will return the following year.

A successful program of class visits means that *every* class of a certain grade in *every* school in your community visits the public library during *every* school year to receive a well-organized orientation to the library's materials and services. Successful programs are approved and even mandated by the school system, because school officials believe in the value of the program as much as librarians do.

Admittedly, this is a big order to fill. You must be absolutely committed to accomplishing this task, and then convince your coworkers, administration, school system (or public library, if you are a teacher or media specialist), and others that the program is worthwhile and essential to the success of the children and teens in your community. We speak from personal experience when we tell you it can be done.

As children's and teen librarians, we feel that now, more than ever, the implementation of a program of class visits is crucial in all public libraries. We have witnessed firsthand the benefits of this true collaboration between public librarians, media specialists, and teachers, and we are committed to its growth and development. This book is the first resource to address this need and to provide a comprehensive guide to help other librarians successfully start their own programs.

The goals of this book are:

- To articulate the reasons and define a strategy for promoting a program of class visits to the public library
- To highlight how a program of class visits can benefit the students, teachers, public library, and the community as a whole
- To provide detailed instructions and easily adaptable templates to assist librarians in initiating an organized program of class visits
- To encourage professionals in both public libraries and schools to seize this opportunity to partner and forge new relationships

For the purposes of this book, these terms are used interchangeably:

- board of education, school committee
- contingency date, emergency date, rain date, snow date, inclement weather date
- library board, board of trustees
- media center, school library
- PAC, Public Access Catalog, online catalog
- Reference Department, Adult Services
- school liaison, school contact
- Young Adult, YA, Teen
- Young Adult Department, YA Department, Youth Services, Teen Services
- youth review board, teen book discussion group

Also for the purposes of this book: a chaperone is an adult, such as a parent or school aid, who accompanies the teacher and class to the public library; a librarian can be either a library professional, a support staff person, service specialist, or aide who is trained to conduct class visits; and a Youth Services librarian can be either a Children's librarian, a Teen Services specialist, a Young Adult librarian, or a (school library) media specialist.

We hope this presentation is of value to you as you either attempt to begin a program of class visits or further enrich your current program. In either case, we applaud your efforts and wish you continued success!

Martha Seif Simpson *and* Lucretia I. Duwel

ONE

How to Get Started

If you are reading this book, you already believe in the value of bringing school groups into the library. Now your job is to convince the rest of the staff and gain their support. Even though the Youth Services staff will conduct the class visits, an endeavor of this size will affect everyone in the library.

Some library directors require a formal proposal in order to introduce a new program or service. Even if your director does not, it is a good idea to get everything down on paper so you can understand the scope of your undertaking. To start, you will need to determine:

• Which grade or grades to target
• How many staff members will be required for each visit
• Who will be your primary contact at the schools
• The class visit schedule
• The estimated cost in materials and staff time
• The benefits to be realized

Targeting a Grade

Many libraries have one Children's (or Youth Services) Department that includes materials and services for all youth from birth through high school. Some libraries have a Children's Department and a separate area and staff for Young Adults/Teens. Deciding whether to conduct visits for more than one

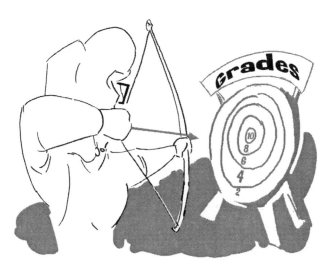

grade will depend, in part, on the number of staff members who are available to do them. The grade level(s) you select will affect the material you present during the visit.

As every parent, teacher, and librarian knows, the abilities of children vary greatly from one developmental stage to the next. We believe that the students' first formal visit to the library should be while they are in the early elementary school grades, kindergarten through grade three, in order to capitalize on their eagerness to go on a school trip to the library. It is a wonderful opportunity to instill a love of reading. Make the trip a memorable one by presenting the children with their first library cards and allowing them to choose a book on their own. If at all possible, try to schedule class visits with at least one of these early grades to get the children excited about coming to the library at a young age. Our own preference is grade two, because students at this level can read well enough to do a simple online catalog search. If that is not possible, at least try to catch the students before they finish elementary school. Don't miss the opportunity to introduce youngsters to the joy of reading and set them on the path to lifelong learning.

Depending on the school system in your town, grades four through nine may be located in the elementary, middle, and/or high school. Likewise, your Children's Department may be designed to serve students up though elementary, middle, or high school. If your library has a separate Young Adult Department especially for middle and high school students, an introduction to this area will provide a good transition from the Children's Department for students who are ready for the next level. Each library and school system is different, and your decision about which grade(s) to invite will depend your particular situation.

Our experience has shown us that it is easier to schedule a series of class visits when the students have just one teacher. For example, if the students in your town move up to the middle school for grade seven, it may seem natural to invite the seventh grade classes in for a formal visit in the Young Adult Department. However, if the students change classes and teachers during the day, it may turn out to be a scheduling nightmare for the schools. Any trips off school campus will cause the disruption of several classes and upset teachers who have to contend with missing students. Whereas, it is much easier to schedule fourth, fifth, and sixth grades, since each class can go as a unit without disturbing another teacher's routine. As an added advantage, librarians can tailor online resource demonstrations to a topic each class is currently studying. In a school system that houses kindergarten through grade six in the elementary school and grades seven and eight in the middle school, our preference is to invite the sixth grade classes to tour the Young Adult Department. We have also found that the sixth grade is a transition year for students, and many are ready for an introduction to the advanced materials and services available to young adults. More discussion about grade levels and what to cover during class visits will follow.

Should your library conduct class visits for more than one grade? It may be possible if there are not many schools in your district, or there are branch libraries that can also do visits. If your library has both a Children's and a YA Department, each area can target a different grade. You must also consider other programming you have in place—can you fit more than one series of visits into your schedule? Another factor to consider when planning the class visits is staffing.

Naturally, if any teacher approaches you with a request to bring his/her class to the public library, you should welcome them. Often he/she will want students to research a specific assignment. You should discuss the details of the project and prepare the materials (print and online) the students will need. This is a good opportunity to introduce your reference services and materials, so that students know they can go to the library to seek help for other classes and assignments. Also impress upon the teacher that you are willing to work with him/her on future projects. (See appendix A for a sample Class Visit Request Form and an Assignment Alert Form.)

Staffing for Class Visits

Libraries, of course, come in all shapes and sizes, from a small building in which a few staff members work in all areas, to large library systems that include several branches with fully-staffed, separate departments for Children's and Teen Services. In your library, consider how many Youth Ser-

"How many staff members will be required for each visit?"

vices staff members are required to provide basic services to your regular patrons during a typical school day. How many additional people, in other departments as well as yours, are qualified to instruct students and are available for class visits? You will also need to consult the Circulation Department to make sure they can handle the additional number of books that will be checked out. It is helpful to have a page or clerk who can expedite the process by bringing the books to the circulation desk, thereby avoiding a crowd of children in that area. Determine if you will need a custodian to open the building early, to set up chairs, or to straighten up the department before the class arrives. Does your library have a separate computer room that needs to be manned? In short, consider the staffing needs of the entire library. (See appendices C and E for Sample Staff Lists.)

Establish a Primary Contact within the school system.

Establishing a Primary Contact

Before you proceed any further, you will need to obtain some information from the schools, such as how many classes will be involved, teacher names, and the number of students in each class. To answer these questions, you should find someone within the school system with the authority to make decisions who will serve as your primary contact and advocate. Although it is possible to call each school individually and arrange for their classes to visit the library, it is much more efficient for you and the schools to enlist one person to coordinate this effort.

Who should your school liaison be? That depends on the administrative structure of the school system, and unless someone representing the schools has approached you to establish a rapport, it may be a matter of trial and error until you find that key person. Obviously, your first call should be to the school media specialists to get them on board with the plan. If the school system has a supervisor who oversees all the media centers in town, that person would be our first choice for the job. Other possible contacts could be the superintendent of schools, an assistant superintendent, the supervisor of elementary (or secondary) education, the head of the English Department, the head reading specialist, a member of the school board, or a board of education secretary. Your school district may have other officials not named here, or perhaps the schools have a well-organized PTA or PTO president who would be willing to take on this responsibility. But whatever your school situation may be, don't give up until you find that primary contact person. It is far easier to work with one knowledgeable person who answers all of your questions and coordinates the schedules for all the schools than to deal with several individuals who only know about their own schools.

By now, you should have in mind the grade you want to invite. Check with your liaison to verify that it is possible to arrange for these classes to participate. For example, perhaps you want to target kindergarten, but your school district has a mix of full-day and half-day kindergarten classes. The buses could accommodate the full-day schedule, but not the half-day morning or afternoon schedules. You don't want to provide visits to only a part of the kindergarten students, so you decide that grades one or two would be a better option. Your liaison can discuss the feasibility of each grade with the various school parties to help you determine the target grade.

You may have determined what you think is the ideal grade to invite for the visit you want to conduct, only to run into fierce resistance from the schools. It is always best to keep an open mind as you venture into new territory.

Let's say everyone has concurred that all second grade classes will visit the library. Your contact will then need to find out:

- How many schools in the district have second grade classes
- How many second grade classrooms are in each school
- The names of the second grade teachers in each school
- The number of students in each class
- The names of the school principals and media specialists in each school
- The school bus schedules and routes
- The school calendar

Once you have these facts, it is time to begin work on the class visit schedule.

Scheduling the Class Visits

Negotiating a class visit schedule that will please all parties involved is a delicate process that involves much patience and the ability to compromise. If you can survive this step, the rest of the planning process will be relatively easy.

Why is the class visit schedule such a delicate subject? Because it requires people to change their established routines, and in this case, many people and many routines will be affected. In addition to the Youth Services staff who will be conducting the visits, you will need people to prepare the library for the visitors, to man the desk for regular patrons, and to check out the additional books borrowed on class visit days. You must take care to devise a schedule that will allow your department and the rest of the library to maintain the standard of service your patrons have come to expect. Likewise, the schools involved will want to operate with a minimal amount of disruption. You and your school counterpart will have to plan carefully to ensure that everything runs smoothly. Since you are both professionals and on good terms with each other, this should be fairly simple to accomplish, right? Let's give it a try.

There are three main elements to consider when scheduling class visits. They are:

• The arrival and departure times of the classes
• The day of the week on which these visits will occur
• The calendar dates for the visits

Each of these elements must be worked out to the satisfaction of both the schools and the public library. Let's examine a few possible scenarios.

ARRIVAL AND DEPARTURE TIMES

The elementary school day typically begins some time between 8:00 AM and 9:00 AM. Most public libraries do not open that early. For our purposes, let's imagine that school starts at 8:30 AM, and the library opens to the public at 10:00 AM. You would like the second grade students to spend a full hour in the library in order to tour the Children's Department, receive a library card, choose a book, listen to a story, and learn about the online catalog. You could begin the class visit at 10:00 AM, but scheduling a class to arrive exactly when the library opens is bound to be confusing and disruptive to the library staff and your other patrons.

We have found it preferable to conduct a class visit before the library opens, so that we can give our full attention to the students and not worry about disturbing other patrons. A class visit that starts at 9:15 AM will give the school bus adequate time to complete its regular route, return to the school, and deliver the class to the library. An hour-long visit would end at 10:15 AM, after the first rush of regular patrons have had time to enter the building. There is a 15-minute overlap when the class and other Children's patrons will be together, but with careful planning, it can be done with a minimal disruption of service. In this scenario, the librarians conducting the class visit would have to report to the library by 9:00 AM to be ready when the bus drops off the class at 9:15 AM.

This plan also requires other staff members to arrive early. You know that the custodian opens the building at 8:00 AM, but will the Circulation staff arrive by 9:00 AM? If the answer is no, you may have difficulty checking out books or processing last-minute library card applications (there are always a few!). A class visit at any time will require adjustments in several routines, but you will need to check with other department heads to make sure employees are, or could be, available to arrive early.

Another possibility would be to start the class visit at 9:00 AM and shorten the time spent in the library to 45 minutes, so the students leave before the general public enters. In that case, your staff should arrive at 8:45 AM to prepare and you would have to eliminate or shorten something from your presentation. Either option will impact the librarians' schedules and your personnel budget, which we will discuss later in this chapter.

If you are unable to schedule a visit before the library opens, it is still best to wait until after the doors open at 10:00 AM. If you welcome the class at 10:15 AM, the visit could end at 11:15 AM, which would generally give the bus driver enough time to return the children to their school in time for their lunch, while keeping the bus on schedule for the half-day kindergarten classes. Discuss these options with your staff, supervisor, coworkers, and of course, the school liaison to determine the best timetable for your situation.

How long should the class visit take? Thirty minutes? An hour? An hour and a half? It depends on the age of the students and what you want to cover during their visit. Young children have shorter attention spans than older students. Generally, 30–45 minutes for kindergarten children and 45–60 minutes for first and second graders is enough time to look for books and do a story time. You may need 60–75 minutes to accomplish your agenda for older elementary school students. Perhaps you can sustain the interest of middle and high school students for an hour and a half, but students are likely to get restless if you keep them longer than that.

THE DAY OF THE WEEK

Let's assume that you have pre-school story time every Tuesday, Wednesday and Thursday at 10:30 AM. On Friday mornings, a part-time music teacher offers a sing-along program. You hold your weekly staff meetings every Wednesday morning before the library opens.

You think Monday mornings would be the perfect time for the class visits. The Circulation Department informs you otherwise. Monday morning is their busiest time of the week since they have to check-in the excessive number of materials that were returned over the weekend when the library was closed. Circulation does not have the time nor the manpower to deal with the additional books that would be checked out during a class visit. The schools also don't like Mondays, because there are too many Monday holidays when the schools are closed. Plus, students (and parents) tend to have trouble remembering things that happen on Mondays, and teachers like to have at least one day at the beginning of the week to remind their classes about the upcoming visit to the library. Thursdays are no good either, because the teachers have staff meetings that day.

The musician volunteer informs you that Friday is the only day she can come. That leaves you with Tuesday or Wednesday, both of which are already booked for story time. It is conceivable that you could move your staff meetings to another day and have the classes come in on Wednesday mornings. If the class arrives at 9:15 AM and leaves at 10:15 AM as planned, you could still do the 10:30 AM story time, but that is just asking for trouble. If the school bus is late, or the story time children are early, you are sunk. Plus, you would probably be too exhausted from the class visit to immediately switch gears and entertain a group of boisterous two year olds. We would not recommend conducting a story time and a class visit at the same time unless you have enough people and program space to comfortably manage it.

We suggest that you ask your school liaison to find out which day, Tuesday or Wednesday, would work best for the teachers and set your schedule accordingly. You will have to move your Tuesday or Wednesday story time to Monday and possibly change the day of your staff meeting, but your story time patrons will get used to the new schedule easily enough. Yes, the Children's staff members will have to be flexible, but you knew at the start that you would have to make some compromises.

Depending on the number of second grade classes in your school district, you may discover that you will need to schedule more than one class visit per week in order to fit them all in. Should you have more than one class in at a time? That would depend on the number of students in each class and whether there is space in the Children's Department to accommodate them all. You would also have to schedule extra staff. Another option is to schedule two classes on the same day, but at different times. For example, the first class would arrive at 9:15 AM and leave at 10:15 AM, when the bus bringing the second class of students arrives. The second class would finish at 11:15 AM. This would require you to conduct the second visit while the library is open to the public.

Another option is to conduct class visits two days per week if your morning schedules will allow it. If, however, there is a huge demand for preschool story time, eliminating one may cause overcrowding in the remaining sessions. You may have to be creative with scheduling, such as holding story time for four weeks with one week off, or providing two story times on some mornings.

Now that you have decided on the day of the week, it is time to set the dates for the visits.

The Calendar Dates

You and the school liaison have agreed that the classes will come on Wednesdays. Take a look at your calendar to determine which days would not be available. Eliminate holidays or other days the library will be closed, days when you will be short staffed (people on vacation, at conferences, etc.) and days when you already

have something else booked. Confirm
the remaining dates with other departments in the library. Make sure that half
the Circulation staff won't be at a work-
shop or that the Reference Department
isn't hosting a debate for the local con-
gressional candidates in the lobby on
any of your potential class visit dates.
Always add two or three extra dates to
the schedule to accommodate problems
such as inclement weather, power outages, computer maintenance, etc. This
will allow for makeup days with buses
already scheduled in the event that you
need them. It is our experience that at

least one of these extra days is used each year. Then draw up a list of the days you
have left and give it to your school contact. He/she will look at the school calendar
and likewise eliminate holidays, vacations, teacher conference days, assembly days,
standardized test days, etc.

What if all 12 second grade teachers insist on bringing their classes during the
month of October, so their children will have an equal opportunity to start the
school year with a visit to the public library? The school superintendent agrees and
the buses are available. It's now or never; you won't get another chance because
the schools already have testing, field trips, and other events scheduled. Should you
try to accommodate them, target another grade, or drop the idea entirely? You
already invested a lot of time and energy into planning for the second grades to
visit, so you don't really want to start the process over again for another grade or
skip the visits altogether.

It's time to think creatively. Perhaps you can take a two week break from your
morning story times and schedule two visits each Tuesday through Thursday. This
would involve more negotiation with the library staff, but it is a possibility. You may
want to offer an alternative program, such as a special Saturday or evening story
time, to appease the displaced preschoolers. Perhaps this plan isn't your first choice,
but you would gain the advantage of accomplishing all the class visits in a short
amount of time while remaining on good terms with the schools.

Once you have a list of possible dates, it's time to assign a specific school and
teacher to each slot. Again, this is best left to the school contact to figure out. Individual teachers may have other conflicts, such as other field trips planned. One
teacher may want her class to visit early in the school year so the students will get
their library cards right away. Another teacher may feel that her students need to
develop their reading skills more to in order use the online catalog, so she would
prefer coming later in the school year. Let the school liaison and the teachers work
out those details. You will have enough to do in the meanwhile to prepare for the

visits. When your school contact presents you with a draft of the schedule, look it over carefully to make sure these dates are acceptable.

Once the dates are set and everyone has arranged their lives (and the school buses) accordingly, be sure to reserve a couple of dates at the end of the list in case a class visit has to be rescheduled due to unforeseen circumstances. (For additional instruction on how to schedule class visits see "How to Schedule a Series of Class Visits" in appendix C.)

Estimating Cost

Many library administrators welcome the opportunity to provide outreach services and forge connections with the local school system, but even the most enthusiastic director will want to know the bottom line—how much it's going to cost. Let's say that the school liaison has told you there are 14 second grade classes containing a total of 322 students. The teachers would like all the students to obtain their library cards before the end of the first school term, so you agree to schedule two one-hour visits per day, one day per week, for seven weeks. Now you can calculate the library's estimated cost for materials and staff.

Determine the cost of materials first. In another chapter, we will discuss letters to the teachers and parents, library card applications, evaluations, and other documents you will need to prepare for the class visits. For now, assume that you will need three sheets of paper per student and teacher. For example:

14 teachers + 322 students × 3 sheets of paper = 1,008 sheets of paper. There are 500 sheets of paper in a ream, so let's say we need two reams of paper. Two reams of paper at $8.00 per ream is $16.00. Also consider the cost of printing. Let's say one printer cartridge is $50.00. You will need to send a packet of

materials in a 10" × 13" manila envelope to each teacher prior to the visit, so compute the cost for one envelope per class:

14 envelopes × $.10 per envelope = $1.40.

Added together the cost for materials is $67.40.

Of course, these numbers and prices are just examples, and your actual figures will be different. You may also have other costs, such as the price of bookmarks to give to the students, or flash cards you make or purchase to help children learn the collection codes. You should not include the cost of any materials that are not specific to the class visit program.

For example, on class visit days, the library will distribute library cards to the students, but library cards are considered part of the daily operating budgt of the Circulation Department. It is unlikely that a public library administration would disapprove of the opportunity to increase their library card registrations!

To estimate the cost of staffing, you will first need to determine which employees—both in and outside your department—will be involved. Next, figure out the number of hours each person will spend preparing for and participating in the class visits. For example: One page earning $8.00 per hour will take about half an hour to prepare each packet of materials to send to a teacher, so:

14 packets × .5 hours × $8.00 = $56.00 for preparation time.

A page will also work during the class visits, which would mean two hours while the classes are in the library plus the half hour prior to their arrival, for seven days. So figure:

7 days × 2.5 hour × $8.00 per hour = $140.00 for class visit time.

Add the two figures together to determine that it would cost $196.00 for one page to complete the class visits.

Don't forget to include all of the librarians preparing for and conducting the visits and the Circulation and other staff members who will report to work early on class visit days. Now that you know which employees will be involved and the total number of hours each will work, you can estimate the staffing cost. At this point, however, you may need to enlist the help of other department heads or library administration, depending on who has access to staff salary information.

By now, you have invested a significant amount of time in discussing ideas with your staff, gathering support from other departments, securing a school contact, negotiating with the schools, and preparing cost estimates. You have obtained factual data such as dates, numbers of students, and staff requirements and built a solid rationale for offering this new cooperative program to the schools. Now you are ready to write a formal proposal and present it to library administration. (See the Presentation Outline in appendix A.) Be prepared to speak to the director, library board, school superintendent, and anyone else to convince them of the importance of this project. Once the proposal is approved, you will be ready to move from planning to production.

TWO

Procedure for Elementary School Visits

In the previous chapter, your department and the schools agreed on which grade will visit the library and how long each visit will last. With your input, the school contact devised a schedule for the visits. The liaison also worked out transportation details from the schools to the library. At this point, your liaison's job is done, and you can proceed.

Now you must meet with your department members and decide exactly what you want to cover during the visits, how you will accomplish it, who will do it, and fit it all precisely into the allotted time. This is when you work out all the details of what will happen once the children step off the bus and enter your domain.

What to Cover During the Elementary School Class Visit

Depending upon the grade level, there are several items you may include during the orientation visits. But for all grades, the most important element is the library card distribution. In the information packets (discussed in detail in Chapter Three) sent to the teachers prior to their visit, be sure to include library card applications for the children. Completed forms should be returned to the library several days before the class arrives, to allow the Circulation Department time to process the cards and deliver them to you. Students who already have library cards should be told to bring them, and you will distribute the new cards during the visit. For the younger grades, the librarian should present the cards as a celebration, along with a talk about proper library behavior. Then give the children time to select a book to check out.

KINDERGARTEN AND FIRST GRADE

Getting their first library card is often the highlight of the visit for kindergarten and first grade students. Although many of them are not independent readers, they have their own ideas about what they like and will enjoy choosing a book. You may want to limit them to a shelf of books you have selected, to make it easier for them to decide. Popular choices for this age include alphabet and counting books, simple concept books, easy nonfiction with big bold pictures (trucks and dinosaurs!), wordless picture books, and stories with lots of repetition or rhyme.

Children at this age will enjoy a story time program that includes songs and finger plays. You can also have a lesson on book care: Why it's important to take care of their borrowed books and return them on time. It is fun to present this by using puppets in a silly skit or song. If you follow story time with a craft or activity sheet, make sure it reinforces the lessons covered during the visit. For example, the children can make a bookmark or color a picture from the book you read. Some author web sites offer reproducible activity sheets that you can use in conjunction with their books. (See Appendix B for a list of author web sites.)

For kindergarten and grade one visits you may include:

- Library card distribution and book selection
- Reading a story
- Songs and finger plays
- A simple craft project or activity sheet
- A skit on how to care for library books
- A discussion about library etiquette
- A game to help students learn where various books are located

"Next stop, paperback fiction."

GRADES TWO AND THREE

Start with a tour of the building for students in grades two and up. If that is not feasible, the orientation should at least include a tour of the department. Point out the librarian's desk where students can ask for help, special areas for programs and crafts, quiet study places, displays and bulletin boards, computers, and other features of the department. Go over collection codes for picture books, easy readers, chapter books, nonfiction, etc., pointing out each collection area and showing children how to read a spine label. Make sure they understand the difference between fiction and nonfiction, DVDs and books on CD, etc. You can also mention upcoming programs which may be of interest and services available to them such as homework assistance, book lists, word processing, and Internet access.

After the tour, allow the children to choose a book. Second and third graders' reading skills can vary widely. Some children may prefer easy readers, while others may be able to handle short chapter books. Popular series fiction and nonfiction presented in a clean, noncluttered format with lots of pictures go over well with these readers. Book and CD sets are also good choices.

By this age, children are ready for a lesson on how to look up materials using the online catalog. For second graders, keep it simple. Go over some basic keyboard instructions and show them how to look up a book by title and author. Use books and authors that are popular and easy to spell, such as *The Cat in the Hat* or Eric Carle. Show them how to tell if the book is in the library or checked out. With third graders, you may want to include a simple keyword search, but to avoid confusion, make sure to use one that will not get too many hits. (Try "ferrets" instead of "dogs," or "popcorn" instead of "food.") You may also want to demonstrate other functions, such as sort list or placing a hold, depending on the time allotted and the students' abilities. It is important to let every child have a turn on the computer. If you do not have enough computers for every child in the class to use at once, you can assign two children to a computer and let them each do one search. If you assign more than two children per computer, they are likely to get antsy and not pay attention.

If there is time, children in grades two and three will also enjoy listening to a story and making a craft. An activity sheet can be given to the teacher so he/she can reinforce the lessons when the students return to the classroom. For example, a matching game that requires children to draw a line from a call number prefix to the type of book it represents will help children remember where different books are shelved. Also tell the children about any upcoming programs that may be of interest to them. (See appendix D for a variety of activity sheets.)

For grades two and three visits, you may include:

- Library card distribution and book selection
- A tour of the department
- A discussion of fiction versus nonfiction
- An explanation of call numbers and collection codes used in your department
- Reading a story
- A craft project or activity sheet
- Simple searches using the online catalog
- Promotions for ongoing programs and special events

GRADES FOUR, FIVE, AND SIX

Although many students have already been to the library by the time they reach grades four, five, and six, you should make sure they have current library cards. Give them an orientation to the department which includes a discussion of reference sources they may need for upcoming assignments. If the teacher has a specific project in mind, show the students some books they could use. You may also

And here's another great book!

show them how to look up materials for their topic in the online catalog and computer databases. When you send your information packet to the teachers, ask if they have a project they would like to research during their visit so you can have materials prepared.

You may want to talk about some new titles and established favorites before you send the students off to choose books. Include nonfiction and poetry as well as fiction titles. If your state has a Readers' Choice Award for this age group, mention some of the nominated titles. Showcase books that will follow the theme of your upcoming summer reading program. Kids will often know about current fad books, but they may not know previous works by those authors or similar titles in that genre. Often, good books that are regularly overlooked will be grabbed by students after you talk about them, so take advantage of this chance to promote quality literature to a captive audience.

Also take time to promote any programs you have planned for students their age. Have publicity fliers, recommended book lists, and other news of interest printed and available for them to take. Let kids know that they can come to the library for help with school assignments, but that you also have programs and materials that appeal to their various interests. The library isn't just for work, but for entertainment, too.

If your library has a Young Adult Department, they may prefer to hold their own orientation for the sixth grade classes. Chapter Four will discuss more ideas for sixth grade and secondary school visits.

For grades four, five, and six visits you may include:

• Library card distribution and book selection
• Book talk about some new titles and established favorites
• An introduction to services available to students
• Advanced searches using the online catalog

- Instruction on how to search online databases and CD-ROMs
- Help on a specific assignment given by the teacher
- A presentation of reference books they will need for upcoming assignments
- A recruitment talk for programs and special events

Whatever grade you target, remember that you will have a limited amount of time for each visit, so don't attempt to do more than you can reasonably accomplish. You also do not want to overwhelm the students with too much information.

Structuring the Class Visit

Structuring the Class Visit

Now that you have determined the grade, how long the class will stay, and what you want to cover, you need to assign time limits for each portion of the lesson.

Let's continue with the example discussed in the previous chapter. The staff members who will be conducting the visits and working the circulation desk will arrive at the library by 9:00 A.M. on Wednesday mornings. You have the list of second grade classes, one per day, and they are scheduled to arrive at the library at 9:15 A.M. Your staff has decided to give a brief tour of the Children's Department, distribute library cards, allow the students to choose a book, read a story, and show children how to search the online catalog. You need to accomplish everything by the time the bus returns to pick up the first class at 10:15 A.M. You are able to schedule two librarians and a page to conduct the visit, plus a third librarian to man the desk when the library opens at 10:00 A.M. Within these parameters, you have to decide how many minutes to devote to each element of the class visit.

The most difficult part to schedule is the online catalog demonstration. First, consider how many computers you have that are capable of doing a catalog search. Are they located together? How quickly do they respond? Can you use all of them or do you want to save some for other patrons to use? Are they in good working condition? If you will be going to a computer lab, is it nearby or do you have to allow for time to walk there and back to the Children's Department?

Try doing a simple title search. How long does it take? How long does an author search take? While you are at the computers, you may want to demonstrate other things, such as reviewing call numbers, checking status, sorting a list of titles, or showing children how to put a book on hold. Practice doing several searches until you find title and author searches that run smoothly on your computers and are easy enough for second graders to do. Add in the time it would take to include additional instruction. It's a good idea to include a couple of minutes to review some keyboard basics before you start searching. Keep in mind that some children may not be familiar with the keyboard and it will take them longer to type out commands. Then add in a couple more minutes of "wiggle room" in case someone shuts off a computer by mistake or the computers are unusually sluggish one morning. How long does it take to accomplish the catalog demonstration? In our experience, it generally takes about 20 minutes to complete this portion of the class visit, but your situation may be different.

Then look at the number of students who will be coming from each class. Let's say the average class size is about 20–24 students. Do you have enough computers for the entire class to use at once? If not, you will need to assign two students per computer, which in this case, means you would need 12 computers. If, for example, you have only six computers to use, you will need to divide the group in half again.

In that case, we suggest that you inform the teacher ahead of time to divide the class into two groups. When the class arrives at the library, assign one librarian to each group. The first librarian will lead Group A to the computers for the online catalog demonstration. Two children will share each computer, with one child doing the title search and the other doing the author search.

Meanwhile, the second librarian will lead Group B on a ten-minute tour of the department. Then distribute the new library cards and give the children ten minutes to find one book. There won't be time for them to check out more than one. (We advise against letting them check out music CDs, DVDs, or software during the class visit, especially if these items have shorter loan times.) Tell the children that after they return their first book on time and in good condition, they will be able to check out more than one at a time, and DVDs, too! Instruct the children to place their library cards inside their books so they stick out slightly, like bookmarks, and leave them on a cart you have handy. While you are reading a story to the group, the page will bring the books to the circulation desk and check them out. By the time you have finished the story ten minutes later, Group A should be done with their computer demonstration and taking their tour of the department. By the time both groups have completed their routes, the page should have returned with all of the checked-out books.

It is a good idea to survey the teachers and chaperones who come with the classes to help gauge the success of your class visit program. Have the evaluation forms ready and ask the adults to take a minute to fill them out before the class leaves. Evaluation forms and sample class visit day schedules are included in Appendix C.

If you have to schedule two classes to come in one day, tell the second class to arrive at the same time the first class is supposed to leave. Chances are there will only be one bus available, so the first class can be picked up after the second class gets off the bus. Yes, the schedule is tight, and your initial class visit may not run as smoothly as you would like. You will discover some bugs that need to be worked out. Perhaps you need to find a simpler computer search or a better route for the department tour, or you discover that the children take too long to find a book. But after a few visits, you will get the routine to run like clockwork. See Chapter Seven for a discussion of some things that might go wrong and how to handle them. (See Appendix C for ideas on introducing call numbers, and on book care.)

Staff Duties

All right, staff, man your stations!

The above example presumes that two librarians, a page from the Children's Department, and one person at Circulation are participating in the class visit. Let's examine the role of each person in more detail.

Staff members should arrive at least 15 minutes before the class is expected to get everything ready. For the online catalog demonstration, make sure the computers are on and working and set up chairs (two by each computer if children will be sharing). Place books, flashcards, and other materials you will need nearby. Set up the area where you will be reading a story and make sure your book is handy. If you choose to do a craft, arrange the materials you plan to use. Pull out books or media you plan to show during the tour and make sure the aisles are clear. Get an empty cart ready to hold the books the children will select. Set out the library cards that will be distributed, along with small pieces of paper and pencils for children who forgot to bring their cards from home. It's a good idea to have some bags available for the checked-out books, to make them easier for the teachers to carry. If you plan to have the adult visitors fill out evaluations, place each sheet on a clipboard with a pen. If you want to give children activity sheets, bookmarks, or other handouts as they leave, count out the number you will need and keep them near the book bags. If you have fliers or other materials for the teachers, make sure you set them out also.

Check the entrance to the library and make sure there is a clear area in the lobby for the class to congregate before you take them to the Children's Department. If there are other library personnel doing their chores, remind them of the class visit so they will be finished vacuuming the carpet, putting out newspapers, moving tables, emptying the book bin in the entrance way, etc. when the group arrives. Look to see that someone is at Circulation to check out books or handle any last-minute library card emergencies.

Just before the class is expected to arrive, one librarian should go to the entrance to wait for the bus. When everyone has entered, greet the teacher and class in the lobby. You may want to draw their attention to the circulation desk, a current display, or other points of interest, but keep it short, because you only have two minutes for the opening part of the visit.

Lead the class to the Children's Department and tell the children where to leave their coats. When they are settled, introduce the other staff members. Have the teacher split the class into two groups. One librarian will start at the computers and follow that routine, while the other librarian begins with the tour.

The page should keep an eye on both groups to see if anyone needs help. Sometimes, the teacher will have a question about a child's library card and the page will have to consult with Circulation. When it is time for the children to select books, the page can assist the librarian in helping the youngsters find what they want. If a child already has a library card but left it at home, write the child's name and phone number on a piece of paper and put it inside the chosen book (or if you can look up the card number, write that down). When the group moves to the story area, the page will bring the cart of books to the circulation desk, wait for the books to be checked out, and bring them back to the Children's Department. Then he/she can bag the books and any other materials you want to give the class, so they will be ready to go when the visit is over. If you want the teacher and other adults assisting the group to complete evaluation forms, the page can distribute them while the students are engaged.

If the visit will still be in progress when the library opens to the public, a third librarian should be scheduled to come in and handle other patrons. This person can also troubleshoot if you have another class visit planned, and they arrive before the first class is finished. The third librarian can meet the arriving class in the lobby and talk to the children about library behavior or book care until the first class has left the Children's Department. That will keep you on schedule, since the two librarians conducting the visits will not have to repeat this information when they take over their groups.

When the instructional parts of the visit are over, each librarian should tell their students to get their coats and line up to leave. The page can collect the evaluation forms and give the teachers the bags of books and other items. One librarian can lead the class to the lobby and wave them to the exit. If another class is waiting, greet them as before and start it all again! (See Appendix C for sample Staff Lists, a Timeline for Class Visit Preparation, and a Teacher/Chaperone Evaluation Form. See Appendix D for activity sheets.)

THREE

Materials for Elementary School Visits

At this point, you have made up schedules and planned the class visits. Hopefully, your school liaison has informed the teachers that their classes will be visiting the library. Now it's time to send them the details and let the parents know. You will need to put together a packet of materials for the teachers that tells them when they will be coming and explains exactly what they need to do to prepare their students for their library visit. It is important to find out the names of the teachers and send a packet specifically addressed to each one. You should also send letters to the school principals and superintendent.

Now is the time to also put together packets for the teachers to take with them when their class visit is over. Materials can include thank you letters, information on library programs, and items for the students. Any activity sheets, evaluation forms, and other print materials should also be designed now.

"...Who, What, When, Where, Why..."

The Pre-Visit Teacher Packet

A packet should be sent to each teacher about three to four weeks before the day of the visit so there will be enough time for the library card applications to be sent home with the students, returned to the teacher, and then returned to the library for processing. Each packet should include:

- A letter to the teacher
- Letters to the parents (enough for every child in the class)
- Library card applications (enough for every child in the class)

THE TEACHER LETTER

The first paragraph of the teacher letter should welcome the class to the library and clearly state the date of the visit, what time the class is expected at the library, and when they will be leaving. If the library has more than one entrance, specify which one they should use. Provide any special directions regarding the bus, such as where to drop students off. Any other details pertaining to the class's arrival and departure should also be given.

Next, discuss any requirements you have, such as parent chaperones, name tags for the children, and dividing the class into two groups.

Then bring the teacher's attention to the enclosed parent letters and library card applications. Explain that he/she should give one of each to every child in the class, collect the completed applications, and return them to the library at least one week before their visit to ensure that the library cards will be made in time. We recommend explaining each section of the library card application in both the teacher and parent letters to avoid any misunderstandings or incomplete forms. Also give directions on what to do if a child cannot return the completed application. This situation may occur if a child is sick and has not been in school or if the child lives in another town. If a child already has a library card, explain that he/she does not need to complete the application and to please remember to bring the card when the class visits the library.

Be sure to mention any other information that is pertinent to the upcoming visit. Also make sure your name, the library's name and address, the Children's Department phone number, fax number, and email address are on the letter in case the teacher needs to contact you. Tell the teacher your preferred method of receiving the completed application forms (via the postal service, in-person delivery to the library, etc.) and again stress that the library must have them at least one week before the scheduled visit. Ask the teacher to inform you ahead of time of any special circumstances regarding his/her students, such as a child in a wheelchair who will be arriving separately or a child who is hard of hearing. Also ask the teacher to inform you of any children who do not speak English and what languages they know, so you can prepare materials accordingly. You may also want to include a note suggesting to teachers how they can prepare for a successful class visit.

Teachers are often inundated with correspondence and other paperwork, especially at the beginning of the school year. If you are starting these visits for the first time, it is advisable to include an explanation in the opening paragraph of the teacher letter that states that this class visit is part of the curriculum, approved by the principal, and *not optional*. This would also inform new teachers that the class visit to the public library is an established practice. Otherwise, you may find that a teacher has discarded your carefully prepared packet (thinking it is junk mail) without reading it! If you are one week away from the class visit date and the teacher has not sent you the library card applications, you should phone him/her with a reminder that the applications must be delivered soon in order for the cards to be ready when the class arrives. If the teacher has no knowledge of the visit, it is better to find out now, when there is still time to correct the situation.

THE PARENT LETTER

We recommend that you start the parent letter by explaining that their child's class will be visiting the public library and give the date. Tell parents that every child should possess his/her own library card and to complete the enclosed application only if their child does not yet have one.

Then give detailed instructions on how to complete the library card application. Do not assume that any line on the form is obvious! For example, explain that the child's name goes on the first line, not the parent's. Inform them about any restrictions on a child's card, such as only being able to check out materials from the Childrens' Department and bring to their attention any boxes to be checked or choices to be made. Instruct parents to return the completed forms to the child's teacher as quickly as possible, so the teacher can forward them to the library.

Tell the parents what their child will be doing during the library visit and that he/she will be able to check out a book. Be sure to include how long the child may keep the book before it must be returned and what the library's policy is on overdue books. Also mention that the teacher will be asking for parent chaperones and to contact the teacher if they want to accompany the class. Remind them that if their child already owns a library card, he/she should bring it on the day of the class visit. Tactfully request that if the child has any outstanding fines or lost books charged to his/her card, the parent should come into the library prior to the class visit to clear them up. As with the teacher letters, make sure your name and all contact information are on the letter in case a parent has any questions.

THE LIBRARY CARD APPLICATION

Obtain enough library card applications from the Circulation Department for each child in the class. If your library has different forms for elementary school students, make sure you pick up the correct ones. If you live in a town where there is a large non–English speaking population, it may be helpful to include applications written in the predominant language and sample forms showing how to complete them.

Some libraries have developed special library cards for local schoolteachers. These cards give teachers additional perks, such as longer loan times or permission to check out a large quantity of books on a particular subject. If your library has a special teacher card, include an application in the packet, as well as a letter describing the benefits of using the card.

The Post-Visit Teacher Packet

Prepare a post-visit packet of materials to give to the teachers as they leave the library. This packet should include:

- A follow-up letter thanking the teacher for bringing the class, explaining the other items in the packet, and providing the due date for the books that the children checked out.
- Evaluation forms for the teacher and chaperones to fill out to help the librarians appraise and improve the class visits. (You can have them complete the forms while they are still in the library.)
- Activity sheets for the students that will reinforce what they learned at the library

"And here are..."

"...some lovely parting gifts for today's visitors."

If you have these available, you can also include:

- Your business card
- A small leaflet listing some of the resources and services that are available for teachers in the public library
- An explanation of library hours, due dates, and fines
- An Assignment Alert Form that teachers can complete and send to you so you will be aware of future class projects
- A calendar of upcoming events that would be of interest to the students
- A bibliography of suggested books owned by the library for this age group
- Bookmarks, stickers, or other materials you want to give to the students

And finally, most school districts have their own permission forms that they require parents to complete for when a child leaves the school campus on a field trip. If yours does not, provide one for them. A sample form is included in Appendix A. Check with your legal advisor to see if any special language should be added.

Other Print Materials

Once the schedule has been set, you can send letters to the principals and other school officials to inform them of the upcoming class visits. Summarize what you will be doing with the classes, include copies of the materials in the teacher packets along with the class visit schedule, and thank them for supporting this valuable relationship between the public library and the school system.

You may also want to prepare other items for library staff to use during the visits, such as flash cards of collection codes, a map of the department, or index cards for indicating the exact time allowed for each part of the class visit.

FOUR

Procedure for Secondary School Visits

Education systems can vary widely depending on geographic location. In some areas, students will attend one school from kindergarten through grade eight, while students in other communities may attend two or three different schools during these years. Middle school or junior high school could range from grades four through nine. High school may include grades 9–12 or 10–12. A secondary school level orientation to the library is best scheduled when students are about to advance their educational level, whether or not it includes a change in the school. Each succeeding academic experience brings additional requirements, and it is beneficial for both students and teachers to become aware of the various resources that the public library has to offer them at that particular stage of their development.

Secondary school class visits, although similar in basic structure to the elementary class visits already discussed, present their own unique set of procedures. Many professionals may even question the merits of bringing middle and high school students to the public library together as a class. However, the reward is that teens who participate in these visits see the public library as a place tailored to their needs. The goals of bringing secondary school students to the library are:

- To increase their awareness of library resources
- To educate them on some of the basic research tools available
- To highlight programs and recreational materials that may be of interest to them,
- To provide them with new library cards,
- To teach them that a library is a place where they can come and ask for help

This final point is the key reason professionals should spend the time and money that it takes to organize visits for this age group. Many teens find it difficult to approach a reference desk or library staff to ask a question or explain a need. If we allow teens the opportunity to come as a group with their teachers, peers, and media specialists to experience welcoming public librarians who are attuned to their needs and interests, they will return. It is a chance for a two-way street to develop which will last throughout their lives. In our experience, if the visit is relevant and interesting, teens will come back that afternoon, next week, next summer and next year.

Once you have decided that your department will provide secondary school class visits, it is vital to establish a relationship with a key person within the school system. This person will coordinate the visits and bus schedules and convince the library director and the schools that these visits will be beneficial. You also need to decide which day(s) of the week the visits will occur and the length of time each class will be in the library. (See Chapter Two for more information on scheduling class visits.) Then you can determine what will happen once the students step off the bus and enter the library. The library staff, media specialists, and teachers will need to collaborate and decide which grade will come to the library and what should be covered during the visit. Then your staff can plan how you will accomplish it, who will do it, and the minute-by-minute details of the visit.

The Middle School Class Visit

For the purposes of this book, we define middle school as grades six through eight. High school will be discussed later in this chapter.

Because secondary school assignments require more sophisticated library research than those in elementary school grades, your preparation and presentation will differ greatly from that of the Children's staff. To determine the content of the middle school visit, you must have some idea of the major school projects occurring during the time period of the visits. Students will remember more of what is said if they know that it answers a particular question or project that they need to address. Keep up-to-date with changes in the curriculum, including state and local initiatives.

We have found that three distinct lessons can be accomplished effectively in about an hour. Decide what parts of your collection should be highlighted and what computer resources should be explored. It is better to focus on a few items that relate well to these students than to try teaching them everything about the library in a single hour. Lessons could include instruction on the online catalog and pertinent databases and a review of the resources of the YA area, including the computers, reference materials and specialized collections.

Time should also be allocated to discuss your programs for this age group. You could provide a sign-up sheet so they can leave their names, email addresses and phone numbers so you can inform them about volunteering opportunities, discussion groups and upcoming events.

The visit should begin with a welcome and introduction of each staff member who will be interacting with the class. Explain to the students that although many of them had visited the library in elementary school, their needs are different now that they are older, and they are now expected to use more sophisticated resources in their assignments. Since this visit will acquaint them with a variety of materials that

"You are now ready to graduate from the Children's Area to the Teen Department."

might be new to them, they are not expected to remember every detail mentioned. But they should always feel comfortable asking for assistance in the Young Adult Department.

Students who filled out library card applications prior to the visit will receive their new cards, and those with expired cards will be able to renew them during the checkout time. It is usually best to have the teachers distribute library cards as they know the names of the students and can accomplish this more efficiently than the YA staff.

Conclude each visit with a booktalk and allow the students time to browse. Librarians can work with teens individually at the computers to help them locate titles of interest. Usher the students to the lobby so they can check out their selections and send them off with the phrase "Come back soon!" You may find that many do return that afternoon looking for the materials you mentioned. The best part is that they have made a valuable connection to the public library and your teen area will be filled with new faces as they graduate from the Children's area to this "more grownup part" of the library.

STRUCTURING THE MIDDLE SCHOOL CLASS VISIT

As mentioned in Chapter One, the timeline of the middle school visit can be determined after you have decided which grade is coming, how long the class will be in the library, how many staff members will be involved, and what you want to cover. Then you will be ready to structure your class visit

Structuring the Middle School Class Visit

and work out a precise timeline for each lesson. It has been our experience that one hour is the optimum presentation time for most middle grade class visits. This can be extended by 15 to 20 minutes to allow for student browsing and checkout of materials. School schedules, such as lunch and bus transportation requirements, will also dictate the length of your class visit time. The school liaison will need to consult the school schedule and the bus company to negotiate a start time. Since most secondary schools begin early and prefer morning field trips, you should consider scheduling visits before the library opens. Remember to be flexible while negotiating a project of this scale. Perhaps the final structure is not exactly what you envisioned, but it could be a foundation to build upon in the future.

Let's examine an example where the class visit begins at 9:15 A.M. and ends at 10:30 A.M., with the library opening at 10:00 A.M. Staff will need to arrive no later than 9:00 A.M. and will conduct the visit for one hour and 15 minutes. With this schedule, it is possible in many school districts to provide two class visits in one morning. With a "piggyback" schedule, the first class arrives at 9:15 A.M. and leaves at 10:30 A.M. when the second class, which has already been picked up by the same bus, is dropped off. The second class will depart at 11:45 A.M. and return to school in time for lunch. Each class will have one hour of presentation time and 15 minutes of browsing and checkout time.

Assume that an average class has 24 students. We have found that with three librarians conducting the visits, we can divide the class into three manageable groups of eight students each. We can then provide three distinct 15–20 minute lessons and cover a substantial amount of information, while allowing students to have interactive, hands-on participation with the computers and the librarians. (Other variations of the schedule are included in Chapter Five.) Next, you will need to determine the lessons to present and the time allotment for each.

Lesson One. Start with a lesson on your library's online catalog. Since the students are likely to know how to do basic title, author, and keyword searches, you can show them some of the more advanced searches. Use examples that relate directly to topics that they are studying in school to make the lesson come alive. Encourage teens to offer search examples and then allow them to search the catalog themselves for their own interests. Shortcuts to finding information and ways to best utilize your online system may also be explored as time allows. As with the younger students, computer skills among the teens will vary. Some students will be comfortable using a computer, while others may have difficulty. Assure students that librarians are always nearby to provide help.

Lesson Two. A possible next lesson could involve the exploration of one or more databases that can help students with their school assignments. These can be research-oriented CD-ROMs, Internet databases, or library-subscribed magazine resources. The librarian who prepares this lesson needs to be aware of this grade's curriculum, types of assignments, and research requirements. Questions to consider include: Are students required/allowed to use magazine articles, CD-ROMs, or the Internet and include them in their bibliographies? If so, how in-depth and current must they be? How should these sources be cited in the students' reports? Is the research paper a key component of the grade and in what subject area? These questions should be discussed with the teachers and media specialists. You should also take this opportunity to explain to students why some online resources are more trustworthy than others and how to determine which sites are best. Make sure you highlight any web sites that will be especially helpful for upcoming assignments. Teens will definitely see the value of the visit if you show them how to research topics that directly relate to their assignments and offer advice on how to find the most reliable resources.

Lesson Three. Another lesson appropriate for your secondary school visit is exploring in detail the materials and programs of your Young Adult Department, no matter how small or large. Give students a reason to return to the YA area by showing them that you are familiar with their needs and interests. Highlight YA fiction, reference, and nonfiction collections, and also special collections such as music CDs, CD-ROMS, DVDs, graphic novels, and magazines. Assemble a cart of current, high-interest Young Adult materials to talk about during this lesson. Be aware of the assigned topics that these students are involved with at the moment. For example, if these are sixth graders doing extensive research on Ancient Egypt, select the best YA reference books, videos and nonfiction materials on this subject to show them. They will be impressed that the library has the resources to answer their needs and that the librarians will help them find pertinent materials on any subject. Young Adult media collections are also a great way to tantalize students with the variety of ways that they can enrich their reports. Videos and DVDs can provide significant information and wonderfully detailed visuals for their projects, and they make subjects come alive, even to the most reluctant student.

This is also a great opportunity to "wow" the teens with a variety of print and nonprint materials. Show them some items that are just plain fun. Choose books that are teen favorites, perhaps titles selected by your teen book review group. Include an array of great books that you personally love and sneak in a line or two about them. And don't forget to add some popular media. Teens are always surprised when they discover that the library owns music CDs by the hottest groups or a magazine on a preferred sport or interest. Better yet is the level of excitement when they discover that they can check out the item using their library card.

If your Young Adult area does not include YA reference and/or nonfiction titles, explain to students where they can find nonfiction print materials suited to their grade level. Teens may be directed to look in the Children's or Adult Services areas, where the staff should be knowledgeable about the academic and leisure-reading needs of these students. Likewise, if nonprint media with teen appeal is located elsewhere in the library, make sure you tell the teens how to find these in-demand items.

Teen volunteers to the rescue!

Conclude your lesson by mentioning your programs targeted to their age group. Teens and their parents like meaningful extra-curricular activities. If your library has a teen volunteer program, this is an ideal time to tell your students how they can get involved. Young adult volunteers can accomplish many tasks and are of extraordinary help during peak times in the Children's Department when the summer reading program is in full swing. Our library has over 100 teen volunteers who help with the Children's summer reading program, and many are recruited directly from the class visits. Students who filled out volunteer forms at the sixth grade visits receive a letter, email, or phone call in May inviting them to attend an orientation to learn more about library volunteer opportunities. Many students who enjoyed participating in the summer reading program as children are eager to help with the program as teens. Teens can also assist with book sales and repetitive jobs such as folding, stapling and collating. The class visit is an ideal time for librarians to get teens involved at the library and to let them know that you want them to return.

THE WRAP-UP

At the end of the class visit, invite the students, teachers, media specialists, and parents to evaluate the program. You will obtain the best feedback by using a written survey that allows participants to anonymously provide their true reaction to the time spent with you. The questions should be simple and brief and take only a few minutes to complete. The information gathered will allow you to continually refine and adjust the visit to the needs of the class. You can ask the participants to complete evaluation forms at the end of the visit or give them to the teacher to administer after the students return to the classroom. If you decide to give the evaluations to the teacher to administer, make sure you explain that it is important to have them filled out and returned as soon as possible. Always provide a stamped, self-addressed envelope and indicate that you look forward to reading their comments. (See Appendix E for sample evaluation forms.)

Another important item to provide at the end of your presentation is a teacher packet with information about your resources and programs. Your discussions with the teacher prior to the class visit will indicate which items you should include. We recommend a simple manila folder containing bibliographies relating to the subject areas of the class visit, programming flyers, and publicity items. A brochure or flyer describing resources for teachers and how your department can assist them is always appreciated. You could also include follow-up exercises for the students, such as scavenger hunts to reinforce the content of the visit and to encourage them to return to the library and retrace their steps. Offer to collaborate with the teacher to put them together and suggest that the students can receive extra credit upon completion. This fosters another opportunity for teachers and public librarians to work together in planning the materials and subjects to be covered during the visit. Some communities have special library cards and policies for teachers that allow longer loan periods and reduced fines. Teachers are then aware of your many collections, resources and programs that will enable students to succeed in school.

After the presentations and forms have been completed, remind everyone to gather their belongings and items to be checked out. Lead the group to the circulation desk to process their selections and prepare to exit the building.

STAFF DUTIES

The number of librarians available to help with the middle school class visits will determine the number of small group lessons that you can provide. Our preference, as indicated in the above scenario, is to have three librarians providing instruction in three different areas. Depending upon the versatility of the staff, you may decide to rotate the students to each

Staff Duties

of the librarians, in which case each staff member will repeat the lesson three times for one class. Otherwise, each group can remain with one librarian who will instruct his/her students in all three areas. Both of these scenarios are workable and successful. The staff will need to determine their comfort level with instruction on a variety of subjects versus the repetition of doing the same lesson over and over—possibly up to six times in one morning! You may also have the option of substituting staff for the second class visit. Naturally, if you do not have three librarians who can help with the class visit, you will need to adjust your procedure accordingly. In the example used for the second grade visits in Chapter Two, we suggested having two librarians conduct the visits and one librarian to staff the desk for regular patrons when the library is open. In the case of the YA Department, you may not need a staff member to watch the desk if this area is not usually busy in the mornings. If your department is small, you may be able to ask a librarian from the

Children's or Adult Services areas to help you. (See Chapter Five for alternate scenarios and Appendix E for sample Staff Lists.)

Whichever you choose, allow your staff time to prepare their lessons and share them with the rest of the class visit team. This helps everyone work out details, become aware of what others are teaching, and coordinate the examples used. Repetition of the examples and subjects for searches across all three lessons is extremely helpful to students. It creates a cohesive visit which allows the students and teachers to discover how the library's resources can relate to their projects and assignments. If each librarian will be staying with one group, the staff then needs sufficient time to practice all sections of the visit and adapt it to their own style.

These details can be worked out among the librarians who are available to conduct a class visit, while keeping in mind any budgetary constraints. You may experiment with several versions of staffing the class visits before a definite format is realized. Our experience has also proven that flexibility is necessary in order to deal with unforeseen circumstances. For instance, a change in the school schedule may force a teacher to include additional students with his/her class, thereby increasing the number of students in your groups. Also, try to schedule a support staff person to handle problems that invariably come up, such as frozen computers or wandering students.

On the evening before the visit, gather all the materials you will need. Select the books you plan to booktalk and place them on a cart, along with any forms, pencils, teacher packets and library cards to be given out. We have also found it helpful to have a bell to ring when it is time for the groups to move to the next lesson. A page can help you prepare these items so they will be easily accessible.

On the day of the visit, all librarians and support staff should arrive at least 15 minutes before the class is expected. Make sure the circulation desk is staffed and the Young Adult Department is presentable. Turn on the computers and open the appropriate programs. Check the cart of materials to make sure everything is ready. Post one librarian at the agreed-upon entrance to greet and guide the class into the library. Welcome teens warmly and express your appreciation for their visit. Highlight the lobby and other areas of the building as you escort them to the Young Adult area. Once there, tell them where to place their coats and belongings. Introduce the class to the staff members who will be involved in the visit and inform them of the three-area rotation format. Assign students to groups.

It is our experience that bus schedules can vary from our timetables. If you are providing for two back-to-back classes, try to have a librarian available to greet the second class should they arrive before you have completed the first class visit. Usually your first class is choosing books or checking out by this time, which can easily be handled by one or two librarians, freeing another librarian to meet the second class. Flexibility is the key to making your situation work. (See Appendix E for a sample timeline and Class Visit Day Schedule.)

The High School Class Visit

Your ability to provide class visits for high school students will depend upon the teachers' needs, the flexibility of your school system, your staff, and scheduling at the library. As students advance in their learning process, assignments become more complex in depth, length, and requirements. The rationale for conducting middle school visits can also

"Introducing in-depth research at your library."

be applied to this next level of secondary class visits. High school students will learn about the resources available at the library that can help them with their academics, as well as programs and materials of recreational interest to them. Librarians should welcome this chance to develop a valuable association between the library and teen patrons which will last throughout their lives.

If you are fortunate enough to have a school liaison person who is willing to organize a group of high school class visits, you are indeed the exception. Because of the variety of schedules for both students and teachers, coupled with the limitation of the class period, it is usually more difficult to plan a schedule of visits for high school students. Should the opportunity present itself, you can adapt the procedures and format laid out earlier in this chapter.

In our experience interest in bringing high school students to the library for instruction is generally initiated with a teacher who assigns a specific topic to be explored. This is an excellent opportunity for the public library staff to establish rapport with an individual teacher. Start by asking the teacher to submit an Assignment Alert Form so you have a written explanation of the project requirements. If possible, request that the teacher come to the library to meet with you several weeks before the visit to get to know him/her better, communicate your philosophy for class visits, and discuss the outcomes he/she hopes to achieve. If a pre-visit is not possible, be sure to phone or email the teacher so that you will be on target with his/her expectations. Spend time going over the resources that you have in the subject area specified by the teacher. Whether the subject of the visit is Greek philosophy, the United States in the 20th century, or American literature of the 1920s, your preparation time will be well rewarded.

After you determine what is needed for the class visit, your next challenge is to set up a schedule that will work for the school and your staff. Timing of the bus, lunch periods, and impact on other classes and activities will be some of the issues to consider. Usually the teacher is aware of these constraints and may have already worked out solutions to most of them. Try to be flexible as there are usually fewer alternatives open to the teacher. Often, if a teacher experiences a successful high school visit, he/she will return and the procedural aspects of the visit will become less difficult with time. Remember that this first visit will allow you to nurture relationships with the teacher and the students which will benefit everyone.

Once you have agreed on the time of the visit and the subject matter, you will need to prepare for their arrival. Gather relevant print and media materials and locate online resources that will aid students' research. If possible, compile a bibliography of materials available at your library to give to the teacher. While the class is in the library, demonstrate how you searched that particular topic, noting keywords used, databases consulted, and other research tips. High school students, especially those who are planning to attend college, will benefit from learning the process of locating reliable information, even if you have already prepared a selection of materials for them. It may be helpful to prepare a handout to guide students through the research process. If you make research interesting by treating it like detective work, teens will retain more and perhaps return to hunt down information on a topic of personal interest.

Use your judgment as to how the class should be divided into smaller groups. Often the teacher will have assigned students to study clusters which will indicate the form your instruction should take. After an introduction to the research process, students may be content to sit at tables and dive into the materials you have provided, taking notes from reference materials and choosing books to check out. Make sure your students know your library's policy for photocopying books and periodicals and printing from online databases.

When it is time for the class to leave, encourage students to return after school to continue their work. Keep the materials used in a readily accessible area and inform other staff members of the assignment, so that they will be able to help the students as needed. (See Appendix B for web sites with curriculum information for secondary school visits and see Appendix E for a Research Materials Worksheet and a Library Resources Finder form.)

The above instructions work best if your library has a designated Young Adult area. If this is not the case in your library, the following chapter may be helpful.

FIVE

Variations of the Secondary School Visit

The purpose of any class visit is to acquaint both students and teachers with the resources, staff, programming, and physical layout of the library. Every public library is unique in its scope, budget, facility, and the community it serves. Ideally, a library has a designated Teen Services area and staff who can offer a secondary school class visit. But this is not always the case. Some libraries may have a Teen collection that resides in the Adult or Children's rooms, rather than in a separate area, or in a space that is too small to accommodate a class. Some libraries may not have any specialized Young

YA or not YA? That is the question!

Adult staff. In these situations, you will need to examine your library's resources in order to determine the logistics of conducting a secondary level class visit.

When examining your library's resources, you need to consider whether or not your library offers:

- A designated YA staff
- A YA collection
- A designated YA area
- A recreational area for teens
- A computer lab

The logistical questions you need to consider are:

- Who will conduct the visits?
- Which department(s) will need to provide staff?
- Where will the visits take place in your library?
- Where are materials for teens located? Are they all in one department or scattered throughout the library?
- How will the visits impact other patrons and departments and the library's schedule?

We believe that the staff members who are most familiar with the needs and requirements of secondary level students are best suited to conduct the visits. If the Adult Services librarians regularly assist with the teens in your community, they would probably be the best choice for the job. However, if the Children's librarians are working with your teens, then this is the staff to be tapped for the program. If you are fortunate to have one or more Young Adult librarians on staff, you have a clear mandate of who will organize your secondary class visit program, even if there is not a separate area for YA materials.

In the previous chapters, we discussed how to set up the class visits, what lessons may be included, and schedules. That information can be applied here, as well. Chapter Four presumed that the library had a designated Teen Services staff and collection area. This chapter will focus on how to implement the program even if your library lacks one or more of these advantages. In an effort to provide possible solutions for a variety of circumstances, we have assembled the following scenarios. Some may hit the nail on the head for your library, while others may provide food for thought and help you to discover your own answers.

"All right, team. Here is the game plan for today's class visit."

No YA Collection or Staff

If your library does not have a designated Young Adult collection or staff, try to involve the staff who usually work with students. You will want to introduce students to the best research materials available. Adult reference and nonfiction are best suited to your high school students, whereas the resources in the Children's Department are generally more useful for grades six, seven, and eight. Ask librarians in these departments to help you select materials to highlight during the class visits.

Discuss with the staff if there are any age restrictions on the circulation of certain collections in your library. For example, in some systems, sixth graders are not allowed to check out adult materials. If policies need to be changed or exceptions made, you must work out these details prior to the class visits.

Be realistic in planning your presentation. Don't attempt to gather every possible YA book, DVD, or magazine from various locations around the library. Pull out a few items and tell the students how they can find other materials that will be of academic and recreational interest to them. Plan to provide a tour of the library and point out the collections that would appeal to teens. Print out a list of high-interest materials and where to find them for the students and teachers. Remind students that they are always welcome to ask you for help if they cannot find what they want on their own.

Finally, determine the best place to physically accommodate the class. Pay attention to the number of students that will be coming and also to the size of the students. High school students are significantly larger than sixth graders and will need more space. If you intend to utilize areas in the Adult or Children's departments, you will need to find out how this will affect their space. Would they need to move any furniture or equipment? How will it affect their regular patrons? If program schedules need to be adjusted, you will have to work out a compromise in order to accommodate everyone.

If it is not possible to use space in another department, perhaps you can reserve a meeting room. Gather a selection of appropriate print and media selections and arrange them on a table. If the class will not have access to computers, set up a PowerPoint presentation or do a live demonstration using one computer and an LCD monitor to display your search techniques on a screen. Provide handouts so the students can follow along and add their own notes.

Limited YA Collection

If your library has a small collection of YA books within another department, you will need to determine the best place to conduct your secondary class visit. Depending upon the grade level, it may not necessarily be in the area where the teen books are located. In general, high school students are more comfortable in the Adult Services area, whereas the Children's Department may better suit upper elementary and middle school students.

Plan to bring the students to view the Teen collection. If the materials are limited (for example, fiction only) have a cart of other teen materials available so students will have a good selection of materials from which to choose. If the space is crowded, the students have to stand, or the group would be distracting to other patrons using the area, you should move to another space where the group can sit comfortably and you can give the bulk of your talk on teen materials and services.

YA Stuff but No YA Collection

If your library does not have a separate YA collection, you can stress that there are specialized YA librarians on staff who can help students find what they want, wherever the items are located. Make sure to tell them where YA librarians can be found (which desk or department) and the hours they are available. A bookmark containing this information can be given to students. (See Appendix E for a sample bookmark.)

As you tour the library, point out areas where materials of interest to teens may be found. Show them where fiction, nonfiction, and media materials are located. It is also helpful to give students a handout with this information. Prepare a cart of YA materials to show students and select an area where you can speak to them with few distractions. You can discuss your teen programs and services at that time.

A Recreational Area for Teens

If your library has a recreational area for Teens, it is the perfect spot to greet the class and introduce them to your programs and services. The relaxed atmosphere lets them know that they are welcome in the library and that the staff is interested in supporting their interests. If YA materials are not housed here, gather some on a cart to present to the class, and if you have enough computers in this area, you can conduct the online catalog and Internet instruction here. Otherwise, you will need to move to another part of the library to use the computers.

A Computer Lab

If your library has a computer lab, reserve it for the class visit. If this will displace other patrons, make sure there is a sign posted that explains why the computers are unavailable and when the lab will reopen to the public. If the lab is regularly used for group instruction, it is a good practice to post a calendar of times when the room is reserved for special use.

You may decide that the bulk of your class visit can be set in the computer lab, especially if you do not have a separate Young Adult Department. If so, work out the details of the individual instruction lessons depending upon the space available. Perhaps the lessons involving the online catalog, databases, and Internet can be done in the lab, and you can move to another area to highlight your teen materials and programs. If the computer lab is staffed with technical specialists, consult them when planning your online catalog and database searching instruction. Ask a "techie" to help you conduct the visit. Let students know that there is a staff member in the lab who can help them if they need assistance.

In your presentation, make students aware of the procedures for reserving a computer, using the Internet or word processor, and saving and printing their work. Tell them if the computers are filtered or not and be clear about the consequences they will face if they access inappropriate Internet sites. Explain any time limits or use restrictions and your policy regarding chat rooms, music downloads, and other Internet use. Let them know how many students can be seated per computer and that you expect them to exhibit proper library behavior. Inform students of any possible fees, such as how much it costs to print from a computer or to purchase a disc on which to save their work. If patrons need a special card to access or print from a computer, tell students how to obtain and use one. Also inform students if they can use their laptops in the library and if wireless Internet connection is available. It is always a good idea to post your computer use rules and to provide a bookmark or pamphlet for students to take with them.

If your library offers computer classes, such as lessons on how to use word processing or how to search a specific database, tell students how they can sign up for a class. And if your library uses computer-savvy teen volunteers to help other patrons learn computer skills, let students know how they can sign up to volunteer.

The above scenarios should assist you in overcoming any logistical problems you may encounter. If your particular situation is not covered here, see Chapter Seven to read about additional challenges to class visits.

SIX

Materials for Secondary School Visits

Now that you have planned the class visits and set up the school and staff schedules, you are ready to prepare the print materials needed for a program of class visits at your library. The materials you will need are very similar to those used for elementary school visits, including pre-visit and post-visit teacher packets, library card applications, and evaluation forms.

"Now, here's the plan..."

The Pre-Visit Teacher Packet

Approximately three to four weeks before the day of each class visit, send an information packet to the teacher. Sending the packet this far in advance allows sufficient time for the enclosed library card applications to be sent home with students, returned to the teacher, and then returned to the library for processing. Each packet should include:

• A letter to the teacher
• Library card applications
• Letters to the parents (optional)

THE TEACHER LETTER

The letter to the teacher should be addressed to the teacher by name and clearly state the date of the visit and the class's expected arrival and departure times. If the library has more than one entrance, make sure that you indicate which entrance is to be used along with any other special arrangements regarding bus drop-off points and parking situations. Include the name and phone number of the person to contact if there are questions or problems.

Next, inform the teacher of any requirements, such as parent chaperones. We suggest that you request enough chaperones so that each student group has one chaperone, assuming that the class will be divided into smaller groups for their instruction sessions. This would mean that three chaperones would be needed for a class that is divided into three groups. One chaperone may be sufficient if both the teacher and school media specialist are accompanying the class to the library. Parents who are genuinely interested in exploring this educational opportunity with their children will contribute greatly to the success of the visit.

It is important to make sure that each student has a valid library card, since they will have an opportunity to select and check out materials. Check with the Circulation Department to see if students in your target grade can register for a library card on their own, or if a parent's signature is required. If the students can fill out the forms themselves, ask teachers to make sure that all applications are filled out completely and legibly. Indicate precisely how, when and where applications are to be returned. Ask teachers to drop off the applications in person at the library or to send them via the United States Postal Service. Also provide directions on how to handle any unusual situations that may affect a student's ability to obtain a library card. Strongly indicate the date by which the applications must be received at your library in order for the cards to be processed in time for the class visit.

Inform the teacher that students who already own a library card do not have to apply for one again, but should bring their cards with them on the day of the visit. This will encourage students to get into the habit of bringing their library cards whenever they visit the library in case they want to check out materials. Your library may also require patrons to use their cards for other reasons, such as reserving computers or printing.

Conclude your letter by inviting the teacher to contact you prior to the visit to inform you of any upcoming assignments or areas of study so you can gear your presentation to these subjects. Also ask him/her to notify you of any special circumstances, such as physically-challenged or non–English speaking students, so that accommodations can be made and there are no surprises on the day of the visit. Indicate that it is your intention to provide the class with the best possible experience. Make sure that your name, the library's name, the Young Adult Department phone number, fax number, and email address are clearly visible on all mailings.

You may also want to include a note suggesting to teachers how they can prepare for a successful class visit. (See Appendix E for a sample teacher letter.)

THE LIBRARY CARD APPLICATION

Since most middle school students will already have a library card, it is not necessary to include an application for every student in the teacher's pre-visit packet. Send enough for about half the class. If your library has a different library card application for this age group, make sure you include the correct version. If your library offers special teacher library cards, include the application in the packet too. See the library card discussion in Chapter Three and the Teacher Loan Card Application in Appendix A for further information.

THE PARENT LETTER

If your library allows students at this age to complete their own library card applications, you may not need to send letters to their parents. Most school systems require parents to sign permission forms before a teacher takes a class on a trip off campus, and that may be enough to notify parents of the visit. However, if you are asking the teachers to provide parent chaperones, it would be wise to include letters informing the parents about the upcoming program.

If your library policy requires a parent to complete the card application for a child, you will need to include parent letters in the teacher's pre-visit packet. As in the teacher letter, include information regarding the date, time, and purpose of the visit. Explain that students who already own a library card should bring it with them and that any fees for overdue or lost materials should be resolved before the class arrives. Mention that students with library cards will be allowed to check out items during the visit. You may also want to briefly state your library's policies on circulation periods, renewals, and overdue materials. Extend an invitation for parents to accompany their child during the class visit and include your contact information in case a parent wants to call you about other concerns.

"Thank you. It's just what I wanted."

The Post-Visit Teacher Packet

At the conclusion of the visit, it is valuable to provide the teacher with a folder that includes bibliographies, Assignment Alert Forms, promotional flyers, and other materials that may be of interest. We have found it helpful to publish a simple tri-fold pamphlet that contains information about our resources, materials and programs that are relevant to the teacher and students. It easily fits into a teacher's lesson plan book where he/she can refer to it to verify your hours, special collections, or how to let you know about an upcoming assignment. If possible, affix a business card with your contact information.

Bibliographies, especially book lists that relate to topics addressed in the curriculum for the grade that is visiting, are also an excellent resource for teachers. If a teacher has informed you of a current or upcoming assignment, perhaps you can create a list of relevant resources to distribute at the time of the visit. Other print items, such as bookmarks and flyers, can also be included in the teacher packet. Encourage the teachers to place some of these materials on their classroom bulletin boards as a reminder to students of the variety of resources available at the library.

Other Print Materials

It is extremely valuable to receive immediate feedback from all participants after the class visit. We suggest handing out evaluation forms and pencils at the end of the visit and allowing the students, teacher(s), and chaperones three or four minutes to complete them. These evaluations can be answered anonymously. Just a few multiple-choice questions can help you determine which lessons are working and where improvements can be made. You can also ask some open-ended questions such as, "I would like the Young Adult Department to buy ..." or "I would like the library to have a program on...." Experience has shown us that teens are quite forthright and will tell you what they want, including food, furniture, and large screen TVs!

Evaluations from chaperones are also valuable in that they provide you with information about your area and collections as seen from a parent's perspective. Some chaperones may not have been in the library recently and are truly amazed at the variety of materials and resources that you have for them and their children. It is an opportunity for you to impress your tax-paying public with the breadth and depth of your department.

If you are short of time, the evaluation forms can be given to the teacher, along with a stamped, self-addressed envelope. Explain to the teacher that the students should answer the survey questions immediately upon their return to school, while the experience is still fresh in their minds. Most teachers are very cooperative and some may even write an extended evaluation with several suggestions as well as sincere thanks for the orientation.

Whichever method you choose, you will find that these evaluations can be helpful when you are making decisions about expanding current collections or adding new materials. The evaluation forms can provide you with the information and statistics you might need to sell the continuation of the program to your director or to make changes in staffing or schedules.

You can also present the teacher with activity sheets, such as scavenger hunts or other extra credit projects, for students to work on when they return to school. Many teachers like the idea of giving the students something that will reinforce the information that they learned during the class visit. This is also an opportunity for you and your staff to work with the teachers to formulate an interesting, provocative project, and foster another connection between the public library and the schools. (See Appendix D for activity sheets and Appendix E for a sample library scavenger hunt and evaluation forms.)

SEVEN

Common Challenges

The power to your building goes out just as your first class arrives!
Three staff members call in sick!
The first bus arrives 20 minutes late!

These are all scenarios that have happened to us and will probably happen to you (remember Murphy's Law!) as you plan, develop and implement your school visit program. Experience has shown us that the best prescription for handling these situations is to anticipate possible trouble spots and have alternate plans. Once your class visit plan is set, it is advisable to stop and take a look at those routine parts where problems may occur. Analyze your class visit program with your Youth Services staff, as well the Circulation, Custodial, Administrative and Adult Services departments. Work together to devise a plan to handle each situation, including the person who is most able to accommodate the change.

In order to assist you, we have compiled a list of some common challenges, along with feasible solutions, quick fixes and necessary adjustments. In many cases, your optimum scenarios are no longer achievable due to circumstances beyond your control, so it is necessary to improvise and make the best of the situation. Remember that your goal is to always provide the best class visit experience possible for the students.

For the rest of this chapter we discuss some of the challenges we have encountered and suggestions on how to overcome them. Keep in mind that problems can arise before and during a class visit. Undoubtedly, you will come across other obstacles that are not mentioned here. Just remember to stay positive and be flexible. With experience, you will discover that you can figure out how to handle any situation that may arise!

"Yes, Billy, this is a lovely self-portrait. But you can't use it to check out a book."

Library Card Applications and Library Cards

Late Library Card Applications

To ensure that library cards will be ready in time for the class visit, enlist the help of your Circulation staff. Perhaps the person processing the cards can assume the responsibility of checking to make sure that the library card applications have arrived at least one week prior to the visit. Establish a clear procedure to follow for problems and make sure everyone involved has the contact information for the teachers and the schools. A reminder phone call is usually enough to get the applications delivered to your library. This will avoid having disappointed students who are unable to check out items during their visit. If the Circulation Department is unable to take on this responsibility, then you must check on the applications yourself and follow-up as needed. As the library card is vital to the satisfaction level of your students, it is worth your time to ensure that this is accomplished for every class visit.

Teachers Who Don't Distribute the Applications

Teachers are very busy people, especially at the start of a new school year, and sometimes things get lost in the mix or are misunderstood. We encountered one instance when a teacher, who was new to the school system, threw out the pre-visit packet assuming it was junk mail! Another teacher did not realize that the class visits were a standard part of the school year and not an optional activity. If you are starting a new program of class visits, inform the teachers that the visits are approved and mandated by the school administration. Your school liaison or someone in authority in the schools should relay this information to the principals, who should in turn inform the teachers involved. If you have an established class visit program with a particular grade, make note of any new teachers. It is worth your time to contact them directly. Explain the reason for the visit and tell them to expect the pre-visit packet of materials. They will appreciate your welcoming them, and you could prevent a potential problem.

Teachers Who Arrive with Applications

We have found that almost every teacher arrives with a few library card applications that students brought in that morning. Generally, this is not the teacher's fault. He/she is always quite apologetic and had been hounding the child's parents for days, so it is amazing that the child brought in the completed application at all! Work out a procedure with the Circulation staff. Hopefully, someone will be able to make the card(s) while the class visit is occurring. If not, perhaps the student can still select a book which can be checked out when he/she returns later in the day to pick up the library card.

Students Who Forgot Their Library Cards

The easiest way to handle a forgotten library card is to have the child write his/her name on a scrap of paper to substitute for the library card. The person checking out the books can look up the child's record in the computer.

Expired Library Cards

Determine with your Circulation Department ahead of time how you want to handle expired library cards. Usually, the card can be renewed during check out.

Cards for Out-of-Town Students

If your library is allowed to issue library cards to out-of-town patrons, the student can register for a library card along with his/her classmates. In some library systems, out-of-town patrons must obtain a library card from their own town. If this is true in your area, you must emphasize to teachers, students, and their parents that the student should bring his/her hometown library card on the day of the class visit. Unfortunately, some students will still arrive without their cards. You and your Circulation staff should determine ahead of time how you plan to handle this situation. You may be able to issue a temporary card or hold the materials and have the student return to pick them up later. Occasionally, a teacher may offer to check out items on his/her own library card. Or perhaps your administration can work out a system that will enable your library to readily access a student's record from another area library. If out-of-towners are not allowed to check out books from your library at all, you should to confer with your library administration and the school system to develop a policy that would not exclude these students. In any case, try to eliminate any barriers that would prevent an eager would-be patron from enjoying your library's resources.

CARDS WITH FINES

Sometimes a student may have accrued fines or lost items on an existing record. Prior to the first class visit, consult with the Circulation Department to determine how they want to handle the situation. If the fine is small, perhaps it can be ignored for the moment, allowing the student to check out a book along with his/her class-mates. If the fine is substantial, a staff member may try calling the student's parent while the visit is taking place to make the parent aware of the fines. If this is not feasible, maybe a list of overdue/lost items can be sent home with the student, along with a note requesting that the parent contact the Circulation Department to arrange a payment schedule. You may decide to let the student choose a book, but hold it aside for a day or two until the problem is resolved. Explain the situation to the teacher. He/she may be willing to check out a book on his/her card for the student to read in the classroom. Unfortunately, if the student or his/her family have a history of accumulating huge fines or losing books, you may have to tell the student he/she cannot be allowed to take out a book at this time. You may want to have copies of your circulation policy and fines schedule available to give to the teacher in a difficult situation. Whatever you decide, make sure your library staff understands the policy and are consistent in implementing it.

"We're on to Plan B."

Staff Issues

ANTICIPATED STAFF SHORTAGES

During the planning stages of your class visit program, you will have determined the optimum staff for the task. Once their duties have been established, identify other staff members to serve as backup. Para-profes-sionals and other associates who are familiar with your department and interact with students may welcome this as an opportunity to contribute to the quality of your program. Train them in the basics and have them observe your staff during a class visit. If possible, construct a class visit team to allow for flexibility and vary the schedule so that no one gets burdened with doing every class visit.

Unanticipated Staffng Shortages

If last minute emergencies strike (and they will), remain flexible. Try not to cancel a visit unless there is an extreme situation, since rescheduling may be difficult. Make sure all members of the class visit team can contact you and each other in case a person who is scheduled to conduct a visit is unable to do so and an alternate has to be summoned. Instruct your staff to call you early in the day if they are ill so you will have time to make adjustments. In the case of a staff member stuck in traffic with a class due to arrive any minute, try to find someone else who is already in the building and trained in the basics of the visit to help out. If you have to conduct a visit with less staff, streamline the lessons as you go and do not try to cover as much material. Explain the situation to the students and teachers and simply state that you are trying to do the best that you can under the circumstances. Teachers and chaperones are likely to be sympathetic and also may be able to assist students with some parts of the visit.

Staff Shortages in Other Departments

Staff shortages in other departments are generally out of your control and may be unknown to you until the class visit is already underway. This is why communication among departments in your library is vital to the success of your program. Make sure all department heads know your class visit schedule so they can inform you if they have a problem. If, for example, a member of the Circulation staff calls in sick, that department may not have another person to expedite book check out for the class. In that case, you may need to cut short your library tour to allow more time for the one remaining Circulation clerk to handle the extra work. Or if the custodian is called away to do another chore after opening the building, you may find that the Children's room was not vacuumed. You will either have to ignore the bits of glitter on the carpet from yesterday's craft activity or find the vacuum cleaner and take care of it yourself. It is always wise to arrive early on class visit days, just in case there are last-minute emergencies to handle.

Staff Arriving Early

If one or more staff members need to arrive early for class visits, this will affect their regular work hours. For example, if your library opens at 10 A.M. and staff is expected to report by 9 A.M. on the day of the visit, a person normally scheduled to work from 10:00 to 6:00 will either have to work a longer day than usual, or work from 9:00 to 5:00. Then you will need to schedule another person to work the additional hour. Flexibility is again required. Similar adjustments will need to be made for every person throughout the library whose hours are skewed on class visit days. Perhaps someone from another department can be persuaded to cover the desk during the class visit so service to other patrons is not interrupted. Regardless of

All aboard!

your solution to these challenges, you will need cooperation from other staff members so everything will run smoothly.

A SMALL STAFF

If you have a small staff, our suggestion of three librarians, a page, plus someone in Circulation may be unreasonable in your situation. Remember that we have provided guidelines that have worked well in our experience or what we consider to be optimum situations. If you are unable to meet these standards, don't give up your goal to provide this service! Work with whatever staff and resources you have and don't try to take on an entire school system at once. Start small. Find one school whose teachers are willing to work with you to experiment with some trial visits. Perhaps you can apply for a local grant to help finance printing or other costs. Recruit library volunteers or people from your Friends of the Library group to help with the tour, read a story, or do an activity with the students. It may take a few sessions to find the right mix of people, lessons, and timing that works for you. Once you have a determined a structure that meets your expectations, then you can expand it to include more schools or grade levels. If you think creatively and pick out the ideas from this book that are doable in your library, then you will be able to implement a successful class visit program, regardless of the size of your library or staff.

AN UNCONVINCED STAFF

In Chapter Eight, we state several reasons for implementing a program of class visits, along with suggested goals and outcomes. A sample presentation and links to information that describes the value of school and public library cooperation are included in the appendices. Hopefully, these arguments can help you convince your coworkers and board members to support your plan. Still, you may encounter staff members who do not want to be inconvenienced, adjust their schedules, or make the added effort to bring large groups of children and teens into the library. You will have to do some major lobbying to convince them. Perhaps you can contact the Youth Services staff from a nearby library that offers class visits and invite them to speak to your coworkers about how the program works in their library. Or maybe you can persuade some of the teachers with whom you have worked before to help you. They can talk to their principals and administrators about establishing this cooperative venture with the public library. The school superintendent can, in turn, approach your library director about the subject. You will have to convince your library associates what is in it for them—besides a lot of extra work!

Computer Problems

COMPUTER MAINTENANCE

Even departments that do not deal directly with the public may affect your class visits. For example, it is important that Technical Services knows your schedule in case a major computer upgrade, such as a migration to a new online system, is planned. You must have advance notice of times when the system may be down in case

"Do you think that will hold it long enough to get through today's class visit?"

some visits need to be rescheduled. You will also need to learn any new features added to the online system so you can demonstrate them to your students. Communication among all departments is essential in order to avoid problems.

COMPUTERS GO DOWN

Instruction on how to use your online catalog is a key part of most class visit programs. As you and your staff prepare for this lesson, consider having visuals to assist your presentation, such as cards showing a book title, author, keyword, various collection codes, and nonfiction call numbers. These can be helpful for students who are unsure about the spelling of certain words. If the system goes down during the lesson, you can use the cards to teach the lesson.

You should arrive early in order to test each computer to be used during the class visit. If one is not functioning properly, you may have time to repair the problem. Otherwise, you will at least know not to use that station.

INTERNET DOWN OR SLOW TO RESPOND

If the Internet is down or slow to respond, plan to use paper visuals instead. When demonstrating a magazine or journal database, have a cheat sheet available to give to students detailing the steps to use to access information on a particular subject. Also have available some magazines which contain articles that may be found online. For example, if the class is studying Ancient Egypt, bookmark relevant articles in magazines such as *National Geographic* or *Smithsonian* to show the class. If one computer freezes during the visit, it may be better to ask the student to double up with a classmate than to interrupt the lesson by trying to restart it. Be sure to note any problems so you can discuss them with your network administrator after the visit.

A COMPUTER GETS TURNED OFF

All staff should know how to reboot the computers. However, if a computer gets shut off by accident during a lesson, it may be simpler to have students move to another computer than to attempt to restart the turned-off computer.

OTHER HARDWARE AND SOFTWARE PROBLEMS

Prior to the class visits, take time with your staff to brainstorm any possible computer problems that may happen. Make sure that your Technical Services Department and/or network administrator are aware of the class visit schedule and know which computers you will be using in order to avoid scheduling nightmares for system upgrades or other events. If your library is just starting to use new equipment, programs, or systems, request that a Technical Services Staff person attend a class visit to observe how the computers are responding and to troubleshoot if needed.

Library Building Issues

BUILDING ACCESS AND BUS SAFETY

When meeting with your school liaison to plan the class visits, discuss the physical layout of your library, including where students will be dropped off and picked up. Be clear in your communications about these directions and do not assume that teachers or chaperones will be familiar with your library. Consider students with special needs, including those in wheelchairs. Make sure everyone knows which library entrance to use, especially if the class is coming when the library is not open to the public. You don't want to have a class waiting outside the library or wandering around the building trying various entrances that are locked. Bus safety is also crucial. Determine where buses can drop off students without interfering

"Yoo-hoo! Over here!"

with normal car traffic and ensure that students have safe access to the entrance. Assign a staff member to greet the class at the door. The best-planned visit will get off to a bad start if the class encounters problems before they even enter the building.

POWER OUTAGES

Make sure all staff involved with the class visits know how to reboot your computers if the power goes out momentarily. Be familiar with your library policies concerning power outages for longer periods of time that might necessitate closing the library. Discuss with your school liaison the procedure to follow if a class visit needs to be terminated ahead of schedule.

BUILDING MAINTENANCE

Before planning the class visits, check with your library director for information about any upcoming building maintenance that might affect your class visits. Projects involving carpeting, painting, wiring, heating and air conditioning can all affect building access and you will need to know ahead of time if certain areas of the library will be off limits for periods of time. Outside building projects involving roadwork, sidewalks, and steps may force you to use an alternate entrance. If so, you must notify the teachers and your school liaison so the bus driver can be informed and your visits can run smoothly.

If a maintenance issue arises after your visit has been scheduled, determine if the visit must be cancelled or if it can be moved to different area of the library. Be sure to notify all staff members of the change. Also notify the teachers, chaperones, and school liaison. You may want to call the teachers a day or two before their visits to remind them of the change if a few weeks have elapsed since you last spoke to them.

"Are we late?"

Transportation Problems

BUS ARRIVES LATE

The bus can be the most difficult piece of the visit since it is the area over which you have the least control. A bus may be delayed due to a logistics problem, such as the students were late leaving the classroom or the driver had to negotiate a traffic detour. During your initial staff training for the school visits, discuss what you would do if a busload of students came 10 or 20 minutes late. Could staff remain longer to complete the visit or must they move on to other duties? If the visit had to be shortened, what would you eliminate from your presentation? With your school liaison, make sure that the bus driver knows the exact time and place for each pickup and when the classes are due at the library. If a bus does arrive late, quickly meet with the teacher to discuss your options. It may be possible for the class to stay a few minutes longer. However, when lunch periods or other bus runs are involved, the teacher may have no choice but to return to school at the scheduled time. If you encounter two or three cases when the bus has not arrived on time, inform your school liaison to determine what the problem is and to work out a solution.

Bus Doesn't Arrive

If the bus has not arrived ten minutes after the scheduled start time, contact the school office and inquire if there is a problem. If you are told that the bus is on its way, ask if the class can stay the full amount of time at the library or if they must leave at the hour indicated on the original schedule. Then inform your staff which backup plan they should follow. If the bus has not yet arrived at the school to pick up the class, decide if there is still time to do the visit that day or if it should be rescheduled for a later date. Occasionally, the bus driver will bring the students to the library on time but not return to bring them back to their school. In that instance, you need to know exactly who to contact, whether it be the school administration or someone at the bus company. The teacher should also have this information in case of an emergency.

Back-to-Back Visits

If you have back-to-back visits scheduled, there may be times when the bus arrives early with the second class. Instruct the staff members closest to the library entrance to inform you when they see a bus dispatch a group of students and to lead the class to a designated area where they can wait until you are ready to meet them. Whenever possible, have an additional staff member available to greet the incoming group and talk about basic information, such as book care and due dates, until the first class is ready to leave. As soon as you can, move your first class out of the area of instruction and into the Circulation area for checkout and departure. Then turn your attention to the second group and begin their orientation.

It is important to make sure that the bus driver or company understands which schools are involved on a given day and when the classes are expected at the library. Then it is the driver's responsibility to pick up the students at their school early enough so they will arrive at the library on time. If the second class is coming from a different school than the first group, the driver has to gauge the time accordingly.

Usually the school liaison will be the one to make the arrangements with the bus company, but it is wise to contact them yourself to avoid any misunderstandings.

CHILDREN WALKING TO THE LIBRARY

If a school is located near the library, the liaison may expect the students to walk, rather than take a bus. Most of the time, this is practical and cost-effective. However, if the teacher has a class of young children and they must cross a busy intersection, we suggest that the class ride a bus to the library. It is better to err on the side of caution, and the teachers will be relieved of the additional worry of facing potential traffic hazards.

Dealing with People

TEACHER DOESN'T LIKE THE DATE

Some teachers may want to time their visit to correspond to a certain research project they are planning. If a teacher complains to you about his/her scheduled date, it is best to refer the teacher back to the school liaison. Any

"Next time we do the tour, remind me not to point out the bathroom."

change may affect the bus schedule or another teacher's plans, and the liaison is better prepared to handle this situation.

UNCOOPERATIVE STUDENTS

During the course of your class visit program, you are bound to run across a few challenging students. These include kids who wander off, are disruptive, refuse to share a computer, can't find a book to check out, demand all the attention, are loud or talkative, talk back, or ask too many questions. And then there are the youngsters who all decide they need to use the bathroom. Experienced teachers and librarians usually have their own methods to regain control of their students' attention. Some people may hold two fingers in the air or clap their hands and require the students to do the same until everyone is quiet. Others may ring a bell, speak in a firm loud voice, or even whisper so their students have to quiet down to hear them. You may have to experiment with different coping strategies until you find what works for you. Children who demand extra attention can be assigned to a parent chaperone so that the rest of the class can proceed to the next part of the program on time. Hopefully, the teacher is aware of the various personality traits of his/her students and will not assign all the challenging ones to the same group. Don't be shy about asking the teacher for help if a student becomes too difficult. As always, patience and a sense of humor can help you survive a less-than-model class.

INATTENTIVE TEACHER OR CHAPERONE

Occasionally, you may have to work with a teacher who does not buy into the concept of class visits and would prefer to spend the time correcting papers, looking for a book in another area of the library, or talking on a cell phone. Perhaps the teacher does not feel needed or has another issue on his/her mind. In any case, you must do whatever you can to get the teacher actively involved in your lesson. Ask the teacher to recommend a favorite book, help a student on the computer, distribute library cards, suggest a topic to explore, or otherwise assist you. Praise the teacher for his/her expertise and thank him/her for helping you. Do not admonish the teacher in front of the students. However, while the students are engaged in looking for a book, you may want to discretely pull the teacher aside and remind him/her that the visit is for his/her benefit, as well as the students', and that his/her cooperation is essential for the program's success. An inattentive chaperone may feel bewildered and not know what to do. Again, guide this person by suggesting specific things he/she can do to assist you and the students. It is worth the extra effort to convince the adults of the value of your class visit program, especially if that person will be returning in the future.

ARGUMENTATIVE TEACHERS

Most teachers recognize that the Youth Services staff in the public library is willing to work with them in providing the best possible service to their students. However, you may come across a few uncooperative teachers. Perhaps they resent being forced to come to the library, misunderstand a library policy, feel they have to defend a student or themselves for some reason, or are just having a bad day. Whatever the reason, encountering such a person is never pleasant, especially if they decide to berate you in front of the students. If possible, pull the teacher aside and have another staff member continue the instruction with the class. Talk in a calm voice, as you would to any other irate patron, and attempt to diffuse the situation as quickly as possible. It may be wise to have another staff member step in to answer any misunderstandings involving library policy, such as why a student with $500 worth of lost books on his record cannot be allowed to check out materials. Do not become argumentative yourself and finish the visit as gracefully as possible. After the visit is over, discuss the situation with your staff and supervisor. Depending upon the situation, you may want to speak to the teacher's principal as well. If the teacher returns the following year, you may wish to schedule another staff member to do that visit to avoid another possible conflict.

STUDENTS WITH SPECIAL NEEDS

Welcome students with special needs and try to incorporate them into the class visit as much as possible, depending upon their abilities. In your letter to the teachers, request that they notify you ahead of time of students who will require extra assistance, so that you can accommodate them. For example, children using wheelchairs will have to be directed to an entrance that has a ramp rather than stairs and be allowed to use the elevator during the library tour. You may be asked to use a microphone to speak to a student with limited hearing. A computer may need to be adapted for a student with low vision or dexterity problems. Students within the autism spectrum may be better able to participate if partnered with another student. Invite the teacher to bring along an aid or the student's parent to help out. You may also want to inform them of any materials you have, such as recorded books or books in Braille, which could be of interest.

NON-ENGLISH SPEAKING STUDENTS

You may find one or more students in a class who do not speak English or have a limited understanding of the language. If the teacher informs you ahead of time, try to find a staff member or someone in the community who speaks the child's language to help with the visit. The teacher may also be able to bring a translator or have another suggestion about how to help the student. Unless the teacher suggests otherwise, allow the student to follow along with the rest of the class. Pair the student with a classmate for instruction on the online catalog. If you are doing an Internet demonstration, perhaps you can ask the student to look up a web site with which he/she is familiar. If your library has materials in the student's native language or about his/her country of origin, make sure you present these materials when it is time for students to select items to check out. You may also want to suggest any materials that can help the student learn English, such as a picture dictionary, English as a second language (ESL) books, or book and CD sets. If your library has any special services or materials for ESL patrons, give this information to the teacher to pass on to the student's family. If your school system has designated ESL classes and teachers, try to arrange for separate class visits for these students—and their parents, if possible—so you can devote special attention to them.

OTHER PATRONS

If you will be conducting a class visit while the library is open to the public, you may have other patrons who will be competing for space and attention. It is important to have a staff member who is not involved in the class visit available to help them. If the patron computers are all being used by the class, a staff member can look up items at the staff desk. However, if a child wants to play games on a computer, you will have to explain that the computers are not available at the moment and offer to schedule him/her to use one when the visit is over. Likewise, if a parent and child are playing with the toys in the Children's play area, you must tell the students that they are not allowed to do the same. Usually, your patrons will understand and will even be impressed that you are providing this service. You may want to let them know which days are booked for class visits, so that they can plan to come to the library at another time.

Managing Library Space

GREETING THE CLASS

If your library has a lobby that is large enough to speak to the class without crowding your regular patrons, you may want to start the visit there. However, if the students are easily distracted or the entrance is very busy, you may be better off with a quick hello and immediately shuttling them off to a quieter area before you begin your instruction. You may have a program room where students can sit on a carpeted floor or an area with tables where the class can sit comfortably. Some librarians prefer to address the class as a whole to introduce their staff, discuss library rules, upcoming events, read a story, or talk about books. Then the class

"Class, can everybody see the computer screen?"

can be divided into smaller groups to have computer instruction, look for books, or do a craft or other activity. Wherever you choose to meet, make sure that distractions are eliminated and the students will be able to see and hear their instructor easily.

A Place for Student Belongings

If your library has does not have an area to store coats, you will need to set aside a few chairs or a table on which your visitors can place their belongings. This is especially important in stormy weather when people may have wet coats or umbrellas.

Areas Outside Your Department

When determining area(s) that will be used for the class visits, consider the size of your groups and the layout of the building. If you will be moving students from your department to another area, such as a computer lab or a craft or program room, make sure that everyone is clear on the route you will take to get there. Allow sufficient time in your schedule to accomplish the room change. Also make certain that any areas outside of your department have been reserved for the necessary times to avoid scheduling conflicts.

Checking Out Materials

In some libraries, checkout of Children's materials occurs in the same room. In this case, make sure to schedule a staff member to do this while the instructing librarians are busy with their groups to expedite this process. Other libraries have one main circulation desk where checkout for all departments is done. If the Circulation area is small or there are not many clerks available, it may be preferable for a page to bring the materials there for checkout instead of having the students crowd the area.

But if you want students to experience checking out books themselves, make sure to consider traffic flow so that other patrons are not disturbed. Students individually checking out books will generally take longer than if one staff member brings all the materials to Circulation at once, even if your library has self-checkout, so remember to schedule extra time if you choose this option. Decide with your staff the most efficient way to accomplish this task.

A Small Library

Some libraries or branches are not large enough to have a room set aside for Children's or Teen materials and services. The few staff members who work there need to be able to assist patrons of all ages and interests. Often, a small library is only open a few hours each week. It may seem unlikely for you to offer class visits, but a small library can perform a great service by providing this program, especially if it is located near a school that has no media center of its own. Since space and personnel are limited, it would be wise to schedule class visits when the library is closed to the public. If that is not possible, you may want to post class visit times so that other patrons will have advance notice of when the library will be especially busy and they may not have access to computers or a librarian.

Other Challenges

HALF THE CLASS IS SICK

Given the time your library and the school liaison have invested in booking the class visits, it is usually not preferable to cancel one since it will have to be rescheduled. However, if a teacher calls you a day or two before the scheduled date to inform you that a significant number of students are out sick and requests a postponement, then it is probably better to do so. Hopefully, you will have an emergency date set aside to use. Be sure to inform the school liaison of the change, since the bus company will also have to be notified. And of course, let the rest of the library staff know so they can return to their regular schedules that day and make the necessary adjustments for the new date. If, however, the teacher calls on the day of the visit, your staff has already arrived, and the bus is waiting at the school, it may be better to go ahead anyway. The teacher may not be pleased, but you also have to consider how this last-minute change would disrupt your library's schedule. Use your best judgment and try to find the solution that will accommodate most of the people involved, since you probably won't be able to satisfy everyone.

A SUBSTITUTE TEACHER ARRIVES

If a substitute teacher arrives with the class, take a moment to introduce yourself and briefly explain the purpose of the visit. Do not assume that the sub knows anything about it. Make sure that he/she remains with the class and takes any materials that you had prepared for the teacher. If possible, provide an extra set for the sub so that he/she can learn more about your library and services. If the sub is later hired by the school system, these materials will remind him/her of your willingness to collaborate with the schools.

NO CHAPERONES ARRIVE

It is preferable to have at least one or two chaperones, as well as the media specialist, to aid the classroom teacher during the visit. However, parents or other school personnel are not always available to come. If you are dealing with a large group or anticipate a problem, try to find another library staff member to be present during the visit to help you maintain order. If the class is divided into two or three smaller groups, you and your staff can usually handle the sections easily enough. But if a student becomes ill or is disruptive, it may be difficult to remedy the situation without another responsible adult present. It is incumbent upon the teacher to remain in control of the class and you should let him/her handle the challenge. At the conclusion of the visit, you may want to emphasize to the teacher the importance of recruiting chaperones for his/her next trip to the library in case another difficult situation arises.

INCLEMENT WEATHER

Be aware of the library's and the school system's policies regarding inclement weather. In most cases, if the schools have a delayed opening or are closing early, the visit is usually postponed. Naturally, if school has been cancelled, the visit will need to be rescheduled to one of the dates you had set aside for this purpose.

EIGHT

The Benefits of Class Visits

You have just read about the tremendous amount of time and effort needed to establish a program of class visits, and you may be tempted to ask, "Why bother?" Our experience has proven that this program provides numerous benefits for the students, the educators, the public library, and the community as a whole.

There are several ways to articulate why your school system and public library should work together to provide a program of class visits. In this chapter, we will describe the benefits, impacts, outcomes, and outputs of such a program. You can select, adapt, and add on to these arguments as you prepare your presentations to whatever administrative boards you need to face in order to gain approval for this endeavor.

Remember that the ultimate goal is to convince the school system and the public library administration to mandate a program of class visits in your community. However, if this goal is not realistic for your situation, then feel free to start small and build up to the level you hope to achieve. You will discover that once people see the benefits of even a limited schedule of class visits, support for the program will grow and other opportunities will open up. (For further information, see the Presentation Outline Appendix A.)

"What's in it for us?"

For Students

BENEFITS

The immediate benefit for students is that those who were not previous library users will receive their library cards and become familiar with the Youth

Services area(s). They will learn that they are welcome to come to the public library to receive help on school projects or to find materials of personal interest. These new patrons will realize that the library can be a place to have fun as well as to learn and will be encouraged to return and bring family members with them. Students who are regular library users will gain new knowledge about the collection.

All students will learn about the programs and services available to them after school, on evenings and weekends, and during the summer and school vacations. They will understand that the homework help they receive at the library can directly contribute to their academic success. In addition to enhancing their literacy and research skills, students often discover interests they want to develop and favorite authors or genres that fire their imaginations. Some teens may decide to become library volunteers or join the youth advisory board. During the class visits, students will see that the public library is a safe, friendly environment where they are encouraged to seek help, develop new interests, and participate in activities that contribute to their growth and self-confidence.

IMPACT

- Library card distribution = new library users return with family members and friends = wider patron base
- Introduction to library = students learn about programs and services = increased library use
- Homework help = students achieve better grades and test scores = students and parents understand the value of libraries and support them
- Realization that the public library is a safe environment offering many programs and services = students participate in library activities = teen volunteers who mentor other children

SAMPLE OUTCOMES

As a result of visiting the public library, students will

- obtain library cards and an introduction to the public library which will set them on the path toward lifelong learning.
- meet some of the public library staff and understand that they are welcome to ask the staff for assistance.
- become familiar with the layout of the public library so they can find the materials they need for academic or personal pursuits.
- discover the range of materials, programs, and services available to them at the public library.

- realize that the library offers [insert here the teen material your library offers].
- learn basic research skills, including how to search the library's online catalog and various electronic databases.
- check out books and other materials for pleasure or for use on a school assignment.
- return to the library with other family members and friends.
- find the resources and materials they need to complete a school assignment.
- continue to use the library in the future to research school assignments and check out materials.
- register for the summer reading program [or you can insert another program].
- sign up to be a teen volunteer.
- become regular library users.

SAMPLE OUTPUTS

Complete the following for your library.
- _____ students in grade _____ will obtain library cards.
- _____ books will be checked out during the class visits.
- _____ students in grade _____ will receive an orientation to the public library.
- _____ % of the students who complete evaluation forms will agree that the information presented during the class visit was useful to them.
- Annual circulation of _____ materials will increase by _____ %.
- _____ students will return after the class visit to continue researching the assignment introduced during the visit.
- _____ % of the students who request homework help will say they found what they needed.
- _____ teen students will complete the Library Scavenger Hunt.
- _____ students will attend a program they learned about during their class visit.
- _____ students will find four or more sources for their assigned report at the public library.
- Use of the library's _____ database, which was taught to students during their class visit, will increase _____ % in the current school year.
- _____ students will register for the summer reading program.
- _____ students will sign up to be teen volunteers.

For Educators

BENEFITS

Most teachers and media specialists already know that the additional resources found at the public library supplement and enhance the materials available in their schools. They rely on public librarians to help their students when school is not in session. Teachers will learn that they can use Assignment Alert forms to request materials to be set aside for their classes so their students will be able to find what they need to complete their assignments. They can collaborate with Youth Services

librarians to create book lists and request that the library purchase materials to supplement the school curriculum. Librarians will encourage teachers and media specialists to visit the public library any time to see what is new and to plan upcoming assignments. Youth Services librarians are also willing to partner with educators to apply for educational and community grants, serve on school advisory boards, and visit the schools to promote library programs. The regularly scheduled class visits will allow teachers to demonstrate to their students that learning does not end when the dismissal bell rings and that the school and library are working together to help students achieve a good education.

IMPACT

* Regularly scheduled visits to the public library = teachers keep informed about library's resources = increased use of the public library by teachers
* Teachers made to feel welcome at the public library = teachers inform librarians about curriculum changes and assignments = improved collection development of public library materials and more efficient spending of library funds
* Teachers learn to use Assignment Alert forms = teachers call library to reserve materials for students = increased circulation and better service
* Teachers' realization that public library serves the same students as the schools = increased collaboration = ability to take advantage of grant opportunities that require school and public library partnerships

SAMPLE OUTCOMES

As a result of participating in a program of class visits to the public library, teachers and media specialists will

- receive a structured orientation to the [insert here the appropriate department for your library] area with their classes at least once every school year.
- keep up-to-date with new library acquisitions and services that can help them and their students.
- become aware of the resources the public library has on a given topic so they can modify their assignments if needed.
- submit Assignment Alert forms to give librarians time to gather materials and resources for students.
- request that public librarians reserve books for their students.
- encourage their students to go to the public library for homework help.
- collaborate with public librarians when creating book lists to ensure that the library owns or can purchase the required reading materials.
- advise the public librarians of changes in curriculum so that relevant materials can be ordered in a timely manner.
- visit the public library when school is not in session to confer with the staff about upcoming assignments.
- invite public librarians to serve on school advisory boards such as the school readiness council or curriculum development committee.
- allow public librarians to visit the schools to promote library services such as the summer reading program.
- consider partnering with public librarians when applying for grants.

SAMPLE OUTPUTS

Complete the following for your library.

- _____ teachers will visit [insert your library] with their classes during the school year.
- _____ % of the teachers and chaperones who complete evaluation forms will agree that the class visits were well organized and helpful to their students.
- _____ teachers will apply for Teacher Loan Cards.
- Circulation of materials checked out on Teacher Loan Cards will increase by _____ %.
- Public librarians will collaborate on _____ school assignments or book lists with teachers.
- Teachers will submit _____ Assignment Alert forms in the current school year.
- _____ educators will visit the public library when school is not in session to learn about resources and services that are available to them.
- _____ books will be purchased by the public library as a result of teacher requests.
- Youth services librarians will visit the schools and talk to _____ classes to promote library programs.

- Teachers will partner with public librarians on _____ projects, such as writing grants, cosponsoring programs, or serving together on committees.
- _____ teachers other than the grade _____ teachers involved in the program of class visits will contact the public library to schedule a visit.

For the Public Library

BENEFITS

Many benefits to the public library are inferred in the preceding impact examples. Increases in the number of patrons, in-house and virtual reference statistics, and circulation of materials are all direct results of this school/public library affiliation. Improved communication with the schools can also generate more efficient collection development and expenditure of public library funds since librarians will make it a priority to purchase materials recommended by teachers. These requested items will be checked out by the students, also increasing circulation statistics. This enhanced customer service means greater patron satisfaction, which in turn translates into support for the public library. Students who have a rewarding experience in the library will grow up to be library users and as parents, will bring their own children to the library. Another benefit of a public library/school partnership is that this relationship may foster collaboration between librarians and teachers when applying for grants, developing projects, or forming committees of mutual interest.

All these situations lead to the positive exposure of the public library and demonstrate its tremendous contribution to the quality of life in the community. A library that has proven to be a dynamic force and essential to the growth and well-being of its community will survive in times of economic downturn. Parents, teachers, and other adults who frequent the library to find materials, programs, and services that meet their needs understand that their tax dollars are well spent. These taxpayers recognize the value of libraries and will support the library by speaking up at budget hearings and voting to fund library projects.

IMPACT

- Reaching students who were not previous library users = creating new library patrons = increased library use

- Teachers encouraged to visit the library = librarians inform them of recent acquisitions and new services = greater use of new resources by teachers and students
- Improved communication with the schools = teachers inform librarians of upcoming assignments so they can prepare materials for students = better customer service and greater student success
- Librarians purchase materials to support the school curriculum or for required reading = relevant collection development = increased circulation statistics and patron satisfaction
- Students whose needs are met at the library = future parents who bring their children to the library = appreciation of and continued support for the library
- Librarians form good working relationships with educators = opportunities for grant partnerships = increased funding and visibility for the library
- Enhanced customer service = greater patron satisfaction = increased public support for the library.

SAMPLE OUTCOMES:

As a result of conducting a series of class visit programs, the public library staff will

- introduce all students in grade _____ in every school to the library's resources during each school year.
- distribute library cards to all students and teachers who participate.
- reach many students who were not previous library users and encourage them to return to the library with their families.
- show students how to locate materials and resources to successfully complete their school assignments.
- open lines of communication with educators which will result in better services to the students and teachers.
- explain to teachers how to use the Assignment Alert form and why it is important for teachers to submit them.
- state the advantages of teachers notifying the public librarians about upcoming assignments and changes in the school curriculum.
- inform teachers about any new services, programs, or materials in the public library that would be of special interest to them.
- invite educators to visit the public library when school is not in session to learn about resources and services that are available to them.
- encourage partnerships with educators, such as jointly applying for grants, cosponsoring projects, or serving on committees together.
- urge educators to serve on library advisory boards and allow librarians to participate in school initiatives.

- solicit comments from teachers, chaperones, and teens about the class visit, library services, or other matters of concern.
- modify the class visit presentations to reflect responses noted on the evaluation forms, to take advantage of updated technology and to accommodate changes in the department and library.

SAMPLE OUTPUTS

Complete the following for your library.

- [Insert your library here] will conduct _____ class visits during the school year.
- The library will distribute _____ new library cards to students and teachers who participate in the program of class visits.
- Librarians will respond to _____ Assignment Alerts and teacher requests.
- _____ items will be checked out by students and teachers who come to the library to ask for help on school assignments.
- _____ items will be purchased by the library as a result of teacher requests.
- [Insert your library here] will spend _____ dollars (or _____ % of the annual budget) on materials that support the school curriculum.
- _____ teachers, chaperones, and teens will complete evaluation forms after their class visits.
- _____ % of the completed class visit evaluation forms will indicate that the librarians are knowledgeable and helpful.
- Public library staff will devote _____ work hours during the current school year to school support services.
- Public librarians will attend _____ school-related meetings during the year.

- _____ educators will participate in meetings or programs held at the public library (other than class visits to the library) during the school year.
- Public librarians will partner with educators on _____ programs, grants, or other initiatives (not including class visits to the library).

For the Community

BENEFITS

As more patrons use your resources, there is a corresponding increase in the value of the money spent on the public library, thereby pro-

"What's in it for us?"

viding more "bang for the buck." This outcome can be graphically illustrated by plugging in the numbers for your class visits. If your program of class visits provides for 20 classes of 25 students to visit, that equals 500 students plus 20 or more teachers, several media specialists and 20 or more adult chaperones who learned about your library and checked out materials. If you extrapolate these numbers into the community, more than 500 families from a variety of social, ethnic, religious, cultural, and economic backgrounds have been made aware of everything that the public library has to offer. Undoubtedly, some of these people were already library users, but for others, this will be their first introduction to your library. These new patrons will mean that a larger percentage of the community population frequents the library, thereby appreciating the value of the town's financial investment in it.

Most library directors know that programs for children bring parents into the library, and this also applies to students who participate in class visits. As this program generates new patrons, there is, consequently, an increase in circulation statistics, program attendance, reference requests, and computer use. Accountants and other business professionals who look at use statistics will declare this endeavor to be a worthwhile expenditure of library funds.

In addition to these financial benefits, a program of class visits creates goodwill for the library among the youth and adults in the community. Students who go to the library after school to do homework or participate in a program are engaged in meaningful activity, and not prone to the problems that can occur when teens are unsupervised. These students are future parents who will bring their own children to the library. In addition, today's students are tomorrow's workers, community leaders, taxpayers, and voters. Providing our students with the resources for lifelong learning and encouraging them to have positive experiences in the library will produce smart, confident future citizens who will be able to make good decisions and contributions to society.

Parents who serve as chaperones for the visits will see firsthand how the library can help their youngsters. Other family members of students will begin to use the library, or become reacquainted with it, because of the child's class visit. We often hear parents say that they haven't been to the public library since they were in school themselves, and they are amazed at the wide range of materials they can check out, the programs they and their children can attend, and the services they can use. It is especially important to welcome these families as new-found friends and encourage them to come to the library regularly. Librarians should seize this opportunity to show parents that their library is a vital and viable asset to their lives.

Townspeople who are already library patrons will also benefit from a program of class visits. Many of the parents have children who will come to the orientation with their teachers, and some may accompany the group as chaperones. Even frequent users always find that they learn something new about the library during the visit. It is also eye-opening for other patrons who happen to be in the library while a class visit is in progress to see how engaged the students are and that the library is providing this valuable service. No one who has actually witnessed a class visit can doubt its validity and impact. Your patrons will affirm their belief that the public library is an educational and cultural focal point of the community. You can then tap these townspeople to become members of your board of trustees, Friends of the Library group, or other support organization affiliated with your library.

Publicizing successful programs at the library makes your community attractive to potential home owners, businesses, and families that may want to move there. A group of students enthusiastically engaged in learning at the library provides a good photo opportunity for the local press. Whenever you conduct any visits for schools, even on a small scale, make sure someone takes pictures. Seeing is believing, and a few well-produced photographs that illustrate the vitality of your program can make a persuasive argument for you to expand your small class visit program to a larger initiative. Also make sure that these pictures are included in your library's annual report and other official documents that are available to the public. You want everyone in town to know that the library is actively involved in the education of its youth, who are the future leaders of the community.

IMPACT

- New patrons = a larger percentage of the population frequents the library = greater value of the town's financial investment in the library
- More students with library cards = more families use the library = increased circulation, program, and use statistics
- Student introduction to library = they are set on the path to lifelong learning = continued use of the library when they become adults and parents
- Frequent users = people recognize the value of the public library = taxpayers support continued funding for the library
- Patrons observe a class visit in progress = library affirms its validity in the community = patrons take an active role in supporting the library
- Publicizing class visits = community looks attractive to potential home owners, businesses, and families = library is a major reason for growth in the community = increased community support = funding for the library!

SAMPLE OUTCOMES

As a result of permitting the public library to conduct a program of class visits, the community will

- multiply the number of children and teens who have library cards and who come for academic and recreational use.
- allow librarians to reach out to families of diverse backgrounds and educate

them about the resources, programs, and services available to them at the public library.

- help the library attract new patrons and thereby increase the number of people who are serviced by it.
- see its financial investment in the public library appreciate in value.
- observe an increase in the library's circulation statistics, program attendance, reference requests, and computer use.
- enable students to form the habit of lifelong learning and take advantage of everything the library has to offer.
- encourage students to engage in supervised, meaningful activity at the public library.
- promote positive values to youngsters who will become tomorrow's workers, community leaders, taxpayers, and voters.
- give lapsed library users the chance to rediscover the exciting resources that are available at their public library.
- affirm the belief that the public library is an educational and cultural asset to society.
- recruit townspeople to join the Board of Trustees, Friends of the Library, or other support organization affiliated with the library.
- publicize class visits to promote the community to potential new home owners, businesses and families.
- provide justification for additional financial support for the library.

SAMPLE OUTPUTS

Complete the following for your library.

- New library card registration will increase by _____ % in the coming year.
- _____ % of the people in [insert your city] will have library cards by the end of the fiscal year.
- Total circulation of library materials will increase by _____ % by the end of the fiscal year.
- Total program attendance will increase by _____ %.
- The total number of in-house reference questions answered will increase by _____ %.
- Computer lab use will increase by _____ %.
- Patron surveys will indicate that _____ % of all library users are satisfied with the service they receive at the public library.
- _____ % of students surveyed will agree that the public library has made an important contribution to their lives.

- _____ patrons will speak at budget hearings to support the public library.
- _____ people in the community will join the Friends of the Library group [or another library support organization].
- Publicity about the library's programs and activities, including class visits, will appear in the local press _____ times each month.
- The town budget will include $ _____ to fund a program of class visits.

A Sound Investment for All

"Small opportunities are often the beginning of great enterprises."
—*Demosthenes, Athenian orator*
and statesman (384–322 B.C.)

As public libraries foster collaboration with the educational system, they nurture the personal development of their youth, support the efforts of their teachers, and establish the library as an essential component of a thriving community. Your library most likely has a working relationship with the schools already. When town budgets are tight, elected officials look to get the best value for their dollars. Encouraging students to utilize the library's resources by sponsoring a program of class visits is a sound economic decision. Now is the time to approach your administrators and advocate for this program. The time and effort you expend will benefit every member of the community for years to come.

Plans and Forms:
Preparing for a
Class Visit Program

Class Visit and Assignment Planning:

How Teachers Can Help the Public Library Help Their Students

How Teachers Can Prepare for a Successful Elementary Class Visit

How Teachers Can Prepare for a Successful Secondary Class Visit

Presentation Outline

Tips for Designing an Assignment

Forms:

Assignment Alert Form

Class Visit Request Form

Class Visit Permission Form

Teacher Loan Card Application

[your library header here]

HOW TEACHERS CAN HELP THE PUBLIC LIBRARY HELP THEIR STUDENTS

The Children's and Young Adult departments at Anytown Public Library strive to provide the best possible service to students and teachers. Our collections contain a variety of fiction, nonfiction, reference and media materials to help students with homework assignments and projects. However, it is not always possible to anticipate the topics that will be assigned during a given school year. Teachers can help us develop our collections and have materials available for their students in several ways:

- Please let us know at the start of the school year if you plan to introduce a subject area that is new to the curriculum, so that we will have adequate time to access our materials, purchase items as necessary, and locate reliable online resources.

- Visit the library in person before you assign a topic to the class, so we can show you the materials and resources we have available. We are happy to work with you and can reserve items for your students to check out or use in the library.

- Fill out an Assignment Alert Form and submit it to us at least one week before the giving the project to your students to allow us time to gather relevant materials.

- Send us a copy of your original assignment or reading list a week in advance. This is helpful in case a student loses or forgets to bring his/hers.

- Apply for a Teacher Loan Card which will enable you to check out several items on a topic for your students to use in the classroom. The normal loan time is also extended for these materials.

- Encourage students who are assigned the same topic to check out different materials and then share them with each other. This will avoid competition for the best resources and foster group cooperation.

- Allow students to use black-and-white copies of articles or pictures, rather than originals or color copies. Our library does not have the equipment for patrons to make color copies.

- Advise students to ask the librarians for assistance. They should not feel shy or think they are bothering us. Tell them we are happy to help them find whatever materials they need.

- Call us if you want to bring your class to the library to do research. We will arrange a time when we have staff available to help you and will reserve the computers for class use.

We would be happy to host the teachers in your school for an in-service day at Anytown Public Library to introduce you to our resources and inform you of our services. Please call us to arrange a date and time.

[your library header here]

HOW TEACHERS CAN PREPARE FOR A SUCCESSFUL ELEMENTARY CLASS VISIT

- Make sure each child has a library card or has turned in a library card application and that the applications have been returned to the library at least a week before the visit.

- If a student is from another town, make sure he/she has a library card that can be used at Anytown Public Library.

- Tell the class why they are going to the library and what to expect there.

- If the library will be open to other patrons while the class visit is taking place, explain to the children that they must be respectful of other library users.

- Remind children how to behave in public places, such as: no running, no pushing, speaking softly, etc.

- Inform the children that they will not be allowed to play with the toys or puzzles in the kiddie area during the class visit.

- If you have any children with special circumstances, arrange for an aid or the child's parent to accompany him/her. If a child requires medication, make sure you bring it along. Please inform us if we need to make special accommodations for a student.

- Divide the class into groups as indicated in the letter from the librarian. Please do not assign all the challenging students to the same group!

- Arrange to have at least one chaperone per group. Explain to them ahead of time that they are expected to stay with their assigned group and help students as needed.

- Each child should wear a nametag. It is helpful if the nametags are color coded to remind the children and adults which group they are in.

- Make sure the class is ready to board the bus when it arrives at the school. The bus company can usually gauge how long it should take to drive to the library, but the timing may be tight.

- If you want to bring your class to the library outside of the scheduled class visit program, please contact us to arrange a convenient time. Because of other scheduled activities, we cannot accommodate large groups without advance notice.

- After the class visit, remind your students to return their books on time. You may want to post the due date on your bulletin board so they won't forget.

- Encourage your students to return to the library on their own or with their family members.

We would be happy to host the teachers in your school for an in-service day at Anytown Public Library to introduce you to our resources and inform you of our services. Please call us to arrange a date and time.

[your library header here]

How Teachers Can Prepare for a Successful Secondary Class Visit

- Make sure each child has a library card or has turned in a library card application and that the applications have been returned to the library at least a week before the visit.

- If a student is from another town, make sure he/she has a library card that can be used at Anytown Public Library.

- Inform students that if they have any outstanding fines or lost books charged to their library card, they should clear these up with the library *before* class visit day. Otherwise, they may not be able to check out materials with the rest of the class.

- Tell the class why they are going to the library and what to expect there.

- If the library will be open to other patrons while the class visit is taking place, explain that the students must be respectful of other library users.

- If your class will be researching a specific topic, make sure each student brings a copy of the assignment, paper and pencils for taking notes, and money for the copy machine or computer printouts.

- If you have any students with special circumstances, arrange for an aid or the student's parent to accompany him/her. If a student requires medication, make sure you bring it along. Please inform us if we need to make special accommodations for a student.

- Divide the class into groups as indicated in the letter from the librarian. Please do not assign all the challenging students to the same group!

- Arrange to have at least one chaperone per group. Explain to them ahead of time that they are expected to stay with their assigned group and help students as needed.

- Make sure the class is ready to board the bus when it arrives at the school. The bus company can usually gauge how long it should take to drive to the library, but the timing may be tight.

- If you want to bring your class to the library outside of the scheduled class visit program, please contact us to arrange a convenient time. Because of other scheduled activities, we cannot accommodate large groups without advance notice.

- Encourage your students to return to the library on their own to continue researching an assignment. They can also use the library for help on other schoolwork or to find recreational materials that meet their interests.

We would be happy to host the teachers in your school for an in-service day at Anytown Public Library to introduce you to our resources and inform you of our services. Please call us to arrange a date and time.

A PRESENTATION OUTLINE

Once you and your staff have committed to providing class visits, you will have to convince other people. This may include your coworkers, library director, library board of trustees, school administration, and officials in your city or town. This presentation should be short and sweet; a five-minute sales pitch highlighting the basic elements of your proposal. If you are comfortable with PowerPoint, you may want to use it. You can also prepare succinct, well-written handouts to give your listeners. For more suggestions on what to include in your presentation, see chapter 8.

Here is an outline to guide you in assembling the points for your presentation:

WHAT:

- Describe your class visit program in basic terms; what students will be learning
- Indicate which schools (elementary, middle, high, parochial, magnet) will be included and the number of classes that will participate
- Highlight the number of students and families that will be reached by this program

WHO:

- State what grade or grades have been selected, the reasons for choosing them, and who made this determination
- Point out that the teachers (and media specialists) will accompany their classes
- If transition grades have been selected, point out the significance

WHY:

- Briefly discuss the benefits of the class visit program for your schools (including the students, teachers and media specialists):
  - Students obtain library cards and an introduction to lifelong learning
  - Students and teachers gain knowledge of the public library's resources
  - Public library materials and services supplement the schools' resources
  - Collaboration between teachers and librarians
- Briefly discuss the benefits for your library and librarians:
  - Forges new partnerships between the library and the schools
  - Increased library card registration
  - Sets a foundation for future library use
  - More users mean higher circulation, reference, and program statistics
  - Reinforces the idea of the library as central to learning
  - Positive exposure may lead to increased funding
- Briefly discuss the benefits for your taxpayers (including the parents):
  - Tax dollars support the library; more people using the library means increased value for money spent

     o Your tax dollars at work; librarians reaching out to schools

     o A thriving library will attract potential home owners, businesses, and families

- Briefly discuss the benefits for your town or city:
  - o Today's students are tomorrow's workers, community leaders, taxpayers, parents, and voters
  - o Students stay out of trouble when engaged in library activities
  - o Informed public
  - o Public library is an educational and cultural focal point of the community

WHEN:

- Explain why now is the time to implement this program:
  - o Students need the library's resources
  - o In times of budget cuts, libraries are more valuable than ever
- Propose that the program start in the fall of the new school year
  - o Indicate that visits will occur during regular class time

HOW:

- Explain some of the logistics—who arranges visits, coordinates transportation, and provides lessons
- Discuss funding:
  - o Sell the program using the "bang for the buck" reasoning; highlight the number of people who will benefit and the value for dollars spent
  - o Include how much money is needed to start the program and to maintain/expand it in future years
  - o Explain how the money will be provided—by a grant, by library, or by other means
  - o If funding is needed from this organization, make a formal request

FINAL POINT:

- Leave them with something to remember:
  - o A significant fact that epitomizes your class visit program
  - o Something that ties in with the library's (or schools' or town's) Mission Statement or goals

TIPS FOR DESIGNING AN ASSIGNMENT

In order to be successful, school projects must be practical and carefully planned. A poorly constructed assignment or one with unreasonable expectations can frustrate the best efforts of students, parents, and librarians. Here are some pointers for designing a well thought-out assignment:

- Give each student a written copy of the assignment. An assignment that is only given orally may be misunderstood by a student. A parent may also misunderstand the purpose or requirements of an assignment if they are not provided in writing. While you are at it, send a copy to the library, too.

- Check that the library has relevant materials that are appropriate for your students' ages and reading levels. Sometimes the only information available on a topic is either too difficult for the student to understand, or too simple to be of any use. For example, a sixth grade student assigned to write a report on Edwin Binney will have a difficult time finding a book when the only biography published about him was written for first and second graders. (Gillis, Jennifer Blizin. *Edwin Binney: The Founder of Crayola Crayons.* Chicago: Heinemann, 2005.)

- Refrain from assigning every student the same exact project or book at one time, since we are not able to carry multiple copies of all titles. Rather, give students a range of choices within a subject area. For example, instead of requiring all students to complete a report on the Greek god Zeus, allow them to choose any Greek god or hero.

- Call us to confirm that we have the resources your students will need to complete their assignments. This is especially important if the topic is unusual or if the information is difficult to locate. For example, before you ask a student to write a paper on an obscure breed of penguin, make sure that such information exists and that the library has access to it. If you have a particular source in mind which contains the answer you require, please let us know what it is us so we can make it available to the students.

- Consult with us when you are developing a book list for your students. We can let you know which books we have at the library. Sometimes we don't own a book that appears on a school list. If there is time, we can try to order it. If the book is no longer in print, we can suggest another title to replace it. We can also recommend recently published titles to spruce up an old reading list.

- Recognize that there is no such thing as a book with exactly 100 pages. Books are printed in signatures of 16 pages, so you will find books with 32, 48, 64, 80, 96, 112, or 128 pages, but not 100! Students who are good readers or who like the topic won't mind checking out a longer book. But other students may not want to read any more than absolutely necessary and are afraid (with good reason) that their teacher will reject a book with 80 or 96 pages. Being flexible about book length will eliminate a lot of anxiety for students.

- Discourage students from checking out every book on an assigned topic, thereby leaving nothing for the students who arrive later. Often, the student will not even look inside the books to see if the information pertains to the topic. Instead, encourage students to look at the table of contents and index of a book to determine its usefulness.

• Give the librarians a copy of any trivia-type questions, as well as information on where the answers can be found. Teachers are not helping their students learn research skills if the questions are so obscure that even a trained librarian cannot find the answers!

[your library header here]

ASSIGNMENT ALERT FORM

You can help us to better serve your students by informing us in advance of class assignments. Please complete this form and return it to the Children's Department by fax, email, or in person one week before the assignment is given so that we may locate materials related to the topic and set them aside for your class. You may make as many copies of this form as needed. Please attach a copy of the assignment for our reference.

School: _____   Teacher: _____

Subject: _____   Grade Level: _____

Date Assignment Given: _____   Date Assignment Due: _____

School Phone Number: _____   School Fax Number: _____

Number of Students in Class: _____   Teacher's Email Address: _____

Brief description of the assignment: _____

_____

_____

_____

Check off the types of materials that can be used:

___ Books   ___ Magazine Articles   ___ Online Databases   ___ Internet

___ Pamphlets   ___ Encyclopedias   ___ Reference Books   ___ Pictures

Note any restrictions or materials that cannot be used: _____

How many sources are needed? _____

List any required sources: _____

Thank you for completing this form. Please attach a copy of the assignment for our reference and contact us if you have any questions or requests.

[your library header here]

CLASS VISIT REQUEST FORM

Anytown Public Library can provide specialized visits for teachers and their classes when advance notice is given. Please complete this form and return it to the library via mail, email, fax or in person.

School: _____

Teacher's Name: _____

Email Address: _____

School Phone Number: _____   School Fax Number: _____

Best time to call: _____   Home Phone (optional): _____

Grade:_____   Number of Students in Class: _____

Would you like your class to have:

_____ A general introduction to the Children's Department

_____ A general introduction to the Young Adult Department

_____ Help in researching a specific assignment. If yes, please briefly explain here:

_____

The library has an active schedule of preschool storytimes and other programs already in place and we will not be able to accommodate class visits at those times. Please refer to our web site at: *www.AnytownLibrary.org.*

Keeping in mind the unavailability noted on our website, please answer the following:

Do you have a preferred date, day of the week, or time of day for the visit? If so, when?

_____

Please indicate within a 2–4 week range of time your 1st, 2nd, and 3rd choice of dates.

_____

Thank you! We will make every effort to accommodate your request and will contact you to confirm a date. If you have any questions, please call us at (000) 000–0000.

[your library header here]

CLASS VISIT PERMISSION FORM

This year, all second grade students in Anyschool will have the opportunity to visit Anytown Public Library with their teacher. A school bus will pick up the students at their school and bring them to the library. The students will participate in a short program given by the Anytown Public Library staff and will be able to check out a book. After the program, the bus will bring the class back to school in time for lunch.

Please complete this permission form and have your child return it to the teacher as soon as possible. Also, if your child does not already own a library card, please make sure to complete the library card application and return it to the school along with this form.

My child, _____, has my permission to participate in the class trip to Anytown Public Library on day of the week, month, day, year.

_____   _____

Parent/Guardian Signature   Date

_____

Daytime Telephone Number

If I am not available in the event of an emergency, please contact:

_____   _____

Name   Relationship

_____   _____

Address   Daytime Telephone Number

I am interested in accompanying my child's class as a chaperone.

_____Yes   _____No

Your school system may have their own permission forms which they would prefer to use. You should check with your school liaison. Also, your district may have some additional legal language which would need to be added to the form.

ANYTOWN PUBLIC LIBRARY
TEACHER LOAN CARD APPLICATION

PLEASE PRINT LEGIBLY   Date _____

Last Name _____ First Name _____ Initial _____

Grade or Position _____ to _____
Dates of School Fiscal Year

School Name _____

School Address _____

City _____ State _____ Zip Code _____

School Phone Number _____ School Fax Number _____

Email Address (If you want to receive overdue/hold notices via email) _____

Home or Cell Phone Number (optional) _____

I agree to obey the rules of Anytown Public Library and to be responsible for all materials charged to this card, including all fees incurred for any overdue, lost, or damaged materials. In the event my card is lost or stolen, I will notify the library. Replacement charge for a lost card is $1.00. This card is valid for the current school year only and must be renewed each year.

Signature of Applicant _____

ANYTOWN PUBLIC LIBRARY
TEACHER LOAN CARD APPLICATION

PLEASE PRINT LEGIBLY   Date _____

Last Name _____ First Name _____ Initial _____

Grade or Position _____ to _____
Dates of School Fiscal Year

School Name _____

School Address _____

City _____ State _____ Zip Code _____

School Phone Number _____ School Fax Number _____

Email Address (If you want to receive overdue/hold notices via email) _____

Home or Cell Phone Number (optional) _____

I agree to obey the rules of Anytown Public Library and to be responsible for all materials charged to this card, including all fees incurred for any overdue, lost, or damaged materials. In the event my card is lost or stolen, I will notify the library. Replacement charge for a lost card is $1.00. This card is valid for the current school year only and must be renewed each year.

Signature of Applicant _____

Web Sites

Public Library and School Partnership Information

Public Libraries

Research and Reference Information

Authors

Publishers

Other Web Sites of Interest

PUBLIC LIBRARY AND SCHOOL
PARTNERSHIPS INFORMATION

ALSCPUBSCH Listserv   Members of ALSC (Association for Library Service to Children), a division of the American Library Association, can join the Public Library–School Partnership Discussion Group. The group has an electronic discussion list, ALSCPUBSCH, which provides an online forum for school and public librarians who are working together or planning to develop joint activities. Subscribers to the list can ask questions, post success stories, or share new ideas.
http://www.ala.org/ala/alsc/alscnews/alscdisclist/electronicdiscussion.htm

ALSC/AASL/YALSA Joint Task Force on School/Public Library Cooperative Activities   This task force of the Association for Library Service to Children, the American Association of School Librarians, and the Young Adult Library Services Association maintains a joint Web site that includes the "Bibliography on School/Public Library Partnerships" and the "Exemplary Web Sites about School/Public Library Partnerships," both compiled by Kate Todd.
http://www.ala.org/ala/alsc/alscresources/forlibrarians/SchPLCoopActivities.htm

Programs for School-Age Youth in Public Libraries   Report of a survey conducted for the DeWitt Wallace–Reader's Digest Fund
http://www.ala.org/ala/yalsa/profdev/DeWittWallaceSurvey.pdf

Together: Librarians and Teachers as Education Partners   Created by Kate Todd, this site has links to activities, system wide initiatives, and standards for planning cooperative ventures between public libraries and schools.
http://homepages.nyu.edu/~kt429/cooperation/

PUBLIC LIBRARIES

Many public library Web sites have information pertaining to class visits or other types of cooperation with their local schools. Here are a few that have captured our attention.

Addison Public Library, Addison, Illinois   The "Teacher Resources" link includes library visit information and an assortment of helpful Web links for elementary school and high school teachers.
http://www.addisonlibrary.org/subpage.aspx?pageId=6

Boise Public Library, Boise, Idaho   Not only can teachers bring their classes to the Boise Public Library, but public librarians can be scheduled to attend school faculty meetings to introduce their services or share information.
http://www.boisepubliclibrary.org/Kids_and_Parents/Teachers_and_School_Librarians/

Boulder Public Library, Boulder, Colorado   This library's teacher's packet includes guidelines for various types of group visits and teacher cards.
http://www.boulder.lib.co.us/youth/teachers/

Cullman County Public Library System, Alabama   Cullman County's site offers information on the services they provide to schools, including group tours, class visits, tips for teachers, back to school/open house nights, PTA/PTO meetings, and story times for after school programs.
http://www.ccpls.com/schoolservices.htm

Farmington Public Library, Farmington, New Mexico   This library offers class visits designed as different "Library Adventures." See their Web site for the Express Check-out Adventure, the Story Time Adventure, and the Topical Adventure.
http://www.infoway.org/classVisits/#

Ferguson Library, Stamford, Connecticut   This site offers "Learning Kits To Go" and information about the library's Purple Bus for kids.
http://www.fergusonlibrary.org/youth_link/kidol/services_educators/services_educators.htm

Hamilton Public Library, Hamilton, California   The Hamilton Public library site provides information on the library's class visit program and resources to support the curriculum.
http://www.myhamilton.ca/myhamilton/LibraryServices/servicesfor/Teachers

Manhattan Public Library, Manhattan, Kansas   This library's Web site explains their class visit policy on one nicely arranged screen.
http://www.manhattan.lib.ks.us/childrens/classvis.html

Memphis Public Library and Information Center, Memphis, Tennessee   See this site for tips for teachers who want to bring their classes to the library.
http://www.memphislibrary.org/childrens/teachertips.htm

Monona Public Library, Monona, Wisconsin   Monona Public Library offers information for teachers, homeschoolers, and other groups on planning guided tours and class visits to the library.
http://www.scls.lib.wi.us/monona/tour.html#visit%20%20Monona,%20WI

Multnomah County Library, Portland, Oregon   This site connects students and educators in Multnomah County with the information resources of the public library.
http://www.multcolib.org/schoolcorps/

New York Public Library   This library's services to teachers include lesson plans, teacher collections and online links to professional databases in English and Spanish.
http://www.nypl.org/branch/services/teachers.html

The Public Library of Cincinnati and Hamilton County, Cincinnati, Ohio
Resources for teachers and parentson this site include educator cards, class visits, and teacher collections.
http://kidspace.cincinnatilibrary.org/teapar.asp

Santa Monica Public Library, Santa Monica, California   The Santa Monica Public Library offers monthly visits as well as single class visits or tours.
http://www.smplkids.org/teachers/libinfo/class_visits.htm

RESEARCH AND REFERENCE INFORMATION

The Big 6   An information literacy model with links to lessons and strategies that teachers and librarians can use to teach research and problem-solving skills.
http://www.big6.com/

The Cooperative Children's Book Center (CCBC)   A research library of the School of Education at the University of Wisconsin–Madison. Web resources include links for librarians and teachers to book lists and author/illustrator information.
http://www.education.wisc.edu/ccbc/about/default.asp

ipl—The Internet Public Library   The University of Michigan School of Information provides this comprehensive resource which offers many links of interest to librarians, teachers, and students of all ages. Check out their "KidSpace" and "TeenSpace" pages.
http://www.ipl.org/

NoodleTools   This Web site offers a suite of interactive tools designed to aid students with their online research and provides the basic building blocks of research in an easy-to-use format.
http://www.noodletools.com/

Web English Teacher   This site provides professional resources for English/language arts teachers and has links to children's and teen literature.
http://www.webenglishteacher.com/

The Youth Online Club   This site, by Shauna Lee De Feyter, offers a Canadian-based online club for kids and ideas for librarians and teachers. There are links to reproducible bookmarks and coloring pages, as well as educational activities and resource information.
http://www.youthonline.ca/teachers/

AUTHORS

There are many wonderful author and illustrator Web sites. The sites listed below have reproducible art that can be used for elementary school class visits. For more author/illustrator information, see the Cooperative Children's Book Center Web site at www.education.wisc.edu.

Brett, Jan	http://www.janbrett.com/
Brown, Marc	http://www.marcbrownstudios.com/
DePaola, Tomie	http://www.tomie.com/
Frasier, Debra	http://www.debrafrasier.com/pages/teachers.html
Henkes, Kevin	http://www.kevinhenkes.com/
Jeffers, Susan	http://www.susanjeffers-art.com/default800.html
Joyce, William	http://www.harperchildrens.com/williamjoyce/homepage.htm
Pilkey, Dav	http://www.pilkey.com/index.php

Roberts, Bethany	http://www.bethanyroberts.com/
Seuss, Dr.	http://www.seussville.com/
Silverstein, Shel	http://shelsilverstein.com/indexSite.html
Wells, Rosemary	http://www.rosemarywells.com/

The authors listed below represent just a sampling of the many young adult author Web sites available that offer secondary school lesson plans and activities for librarians and teachers.

Crutcher, Chris	http://www.chriscrutcher.com/
Hobbs, Will	http://www.willhobbsauthor.com/
Yolen, Jane	http://www.janeyolen.com/

PUBLISHERS

The publisher Web sites listed below offer reproducible art that can be used for elementary school class visits.

Candlewick Press
http://www.candlewick.com/authill.asp?b=Author&pg=1&m=actlist&a=&id=0&pix=n

HarperCollins Children's Books
http://www.harperchildrens.com/hch/

HarperCollins I Can Read Books
http://www.icanread.com/

Hachette Book Group USA
http://www.twbookmark.com/children/activity_center.html#printable
http://www.twbookmark.com/children/educator_resources.html

Holiday House
http://www.holidayhouse.com/

Houghton Mifflin   This site offersactivities about Mike Mulligan, David Macaulay's books, and other favorites.
http://www.houghtonmifflinbooks.com/librarians/teacher.shtml

Random House   This site offers links to popular series such as the Berenstain Bears and Dora the Explorer.
http://www.randomhouse.com/kids/index.pperl

Scholastic   This site offers links to many popular series such as Captain Underpants, Clifford the Big Red Dog, and the Magic School Bus.
http://scholastic.com/
Also check out Scholastic's teachers page which offers free resources for the classroom.
http://teacher.Scholastic.com/index.asp

OTHER WEB SITES OF INTEREST

Kay E. Vandergrift's Special Interest Page   Sponsored by Rutgers University's School of Communication, Information, and Library Services, this site by Professor Emerita Kay E. Vandergrift includes links to critical information on children's and young adult literature. It also contains curriculum suggestions and academic discussions on special literature interests such as feminism, intellectual freedom, and culture in children's/YA literature.
http://www.scils.rutgers.edu/~kvander/

Nancy Keane's Booktalks—Quick and Simple   You can find booktalks by title, subject or interest level, and tips on how to use booktalks in the library classroom.
http://www.nancykeane.com/booktalks/default.htm

No Flying No Tights   This site offers information about graphic novels for kids and teens. Click on "give me more" to find Web sites of interest to librarians and teachers, including graphic novel authors/illustrators, resources, reviews and booklists.
http://www.noflyingnotights.com/index.html

Planet Esmé   Author Esmé Raji Codell's website has links to book recommendations and teacher links.
http://www.planetesme.com

Random House   Resources include links to teacher guides for children's and young adult books by title, grade, theme, discipline, or time period, plus information on authors and awards.
http://www.randomhouse.com/teachers/

The Summit of School Libraries   This groundbreaking conference was held in Toronto in May 2002. You can view the program notes at this website, including the full PowerPoint presentation by Dr. Ross Todd, Associate Professor, Department of Library and Information Science at Rutgers University.
http://www.accessola.com/summit/

Plans, Letters, and Forms: Elementary School Class Visits

Planning:

Class Visit Day Schedule

Class Visit Day Schedule Short Version

How to Schedule a Series of Class Visits

Ideas for Teaching Book Responsibility

Ideas for Teaching Call Numbers

Sample Staff Lists

Timeline for Class Visit Preparation

Child Library Card Application

Letters and Forms:

Parent Letter

Principal Letter

Teacher Letter

Teacher/Chaperone Evaluation Form

Teacher Follow-up Letter

CLASS VISIT DAY SCHEDULE

9:15–9:17	*The class arrives and the librarian:*

                • Greets class in lobby
                • Points out the circulation desk and tells what happens there
                • Moves class to the Children's Department

9:17–9:20   *In the Children's Department:*
                • Librarian tells class where to place coats
                • Librarian introduces Children's staff
                • Teacher divides class into two groups

GROUP A:

9:20–9:40   Library terms and collection codes discussed
                Librarian leads online catalog demonstration

9:40–9:50   Librarian leads group on a tour of the department

9:50–10:00   Library card distribution
                Children select one book

10:00–10:10   Librarian brings class into Program Room and reads a story
                Page gives evaluation forms to teachers
                Page brings books to circulation desk to be checked out

10:10–10:15   Class puts on coats
                Page collects completed evaluation forms
                Page gives books and post-visit packet to teacher
                Librarian brings class to lobby to exit

GROUP B:

9:20–9:30   Librarian leads group on a tour of the department and discusses library terms and collection codes

9:30–9:40   Library card distribution
                Children select one book

9:40–9:50   Librarian brings class into Program Room and reads a story
                Page brings books to circulation desk to be checked out

9:50–10:10   Librarian leads online catalog demonstration
                Page gives evaluation forms to teachers

10:10–10:15   Class puts on coats
                Page collects completed evaluation forms
                Page gives books and post-visit packet to teacher
                Librarian brings class to lobby to exit

CLASS VISIT DAY SCHEDULE
SHORT VERSION

(*Note:* This version is designed to fit on a 3" × 5" index card. Group A goes on one side of card, Group B on the other side. You can keep this in your pocket during the class visit to check your time.)

GROUP A:

9:15–9:17   Greet class in lobby, move to Children's Department

9:17–9:20   Remove coats, introduce Children's staff, split into two groups

9:20–9:40   Library terms, online catalog demonstration

9:40–9:50   Tour department

9:50–10:00   Library card distribution and book selection

10:00–10:10 Read story, teacher evaluation forms

10:10–10:15 Get coats, get completed forms, give books to teachers, exit

---

GROUP B:

9:15–9:17   Greet class in lobby, move to Children's Department

9:17–9:20   Remove coats, introduce Children's staff, split into two groups

9:20–9:30   Tour department while discussing collection codes

9:30–9:40   Library card distribution and book selection

9:40–9:50   Read story

9:50–10:10   Online catalog demonstration, teacher evaluation forms

10:10–10:15 Get coats, get completed forms, give books to teachers, exit

How to Schedule a Series
of Class Visits

Even if your school liaison will be taking on the task of assigning school visit dates, you should be familiar with the process. This exercise will take you through the steps so you will understand some of the challenges that may arise.

Assumptions

- This is the 2008-2009 school year.

- You will be conducting visits for all 12 second grade classes in the school system.

- There are five schools in your town: Washington School has two second grade classes, Adams School has five, Jefferson School has four, and Madison School has one.

- Class visits will start the first week of October 2008 to give teachers all of September to get to know their students.

- All class visits will start on Wednesday mornings at 9:15 AM.

- The Wednesdays from October through December 2008 are as follows: October 1, 8, 15, 22, 29; November 5, 12, 19, 26; and December 3, 10, 17, 24, 31.

Scenario #1

In this scenario we will schedule 12 class visits, one per day. There are 14 Wednesdays from October through December 2008 and that should be enough for all 12 classes, plus two contingency dates (or "snow days" if your area gets snow in the winter). However, the schools cannot schedule class visits on the following days:

- October 1 is Rosh Hashanah, the Jewish New Year. Several students and teachers will not be in school that day. (In some school systems, school is canceled entirely.)

- There is mandatory statewide testing for all second grade students on October 22.

- November 5 is a half day so parents can meet with teachers to discuss their children's report cards. The bus schedule is too tight to allow runs to the library.

- November 26 is a half day of school, since it is the day before Thanksgiving.

- December 24 is Christmas Eve and there is no school that day.

- December 31 is New Year's Eve and there is no school that day.

That leaves you with eight possible days, making it necessary to schedule some dates in 2009. Wednesdays for the next three months are: January 7, 14, 21, 28; February 4, 11, 18, 25; and March 4, 11, 18, 25. Again, you will have to discard some dates:

- Your town has designated the week of January 5 as School Safety Week. The schools have activities and assemblies all week, so you can't schedule a visit on January 7.

- Winter vacation is the week of February 16, so you must discard February 18.

- There is mandatory statewide testing for all students during the week of March 9, so you can't schedule a visit on March 11.

After you take away the dates that won't work for the schools, you are left with: October 8, 15, 29; November 12, 19; December 3, 10, 17; January 14, 21, 28; February 4, 11, 25; and March 4, 18, 25.

Now look at your library schedule. You know you will be short staffed on October 8 because someone is on vacation that week and on January 28 you will be attending a library conference. If you have other staff members to cover these dates, you may still be able to conduct class visits, but for now, assume that these days are out. Also, the library will be closed a few days at the beginning of January to install new carpets. You don't have the exact dates yet, but you decide to take out January 14, just in case. This leaves you with: October 15, 29; November 12, 19; December 3, 10, 17; January 21; February 4, 11, 25; and March 4, 18, 25.

Hopefully, there are no more problems with the 15 dates that are left. You can send this list to the school liaison so he/she can assign teachers and their classes to exact days. But just in case you find yourself handling this task, let's try to create a schedule.

You may think it is a simple matter to randomly assign teachers to dates, but it is likely that there are other variables to add to the mix. Such as:

- The teachers at Jefferson School want their classes to go to the library as early in the school year as possible.

- Teacher A at Jefferson School has another field trip planned for October 15.

- The teachers at Washington School want their classes scheduled one after the other, since the teachers plan their lessons together.

- The Adams School book fair is on January 21. The school day is already disrupted, and the teachers do not want to contend with a class visit then.

- Madison School's spring concert is on March 27 and the second grade will have to rehearse on March 25, so they can't visit the library that day.

Even with these restrictions, there are still many ways you can schedule the classes. Rather than making up teacher names, let's just call them A, B, etc. in the following example:

October 15, 2008—Jefferson B

October 29, 2008—Jefferson C

November 12, 2008—Jefferson D

November 19, 2008—Jefferson A

December 3, 2008—Washington A

December 10, 2008—Washington B

December 17, 2008—Adams A

January 21, 2009—Madison A

February 4, 2009—Adams B

February 11, 2009—Adams C

February 25, 2009—Adams D

March 4, 2009—Adams E

March 18, 2009—Contingency Date

March 25, 2009—Contingency Date (but not for Madison A)

Scenario #2

In this scenario we will schedule 12 class visits, two per day. Using the same restrictions listed previously, let's schedule the visits two back-to-back each day, at 9:15 AM and 10:15 AM. We'll add some more variables as well:

- Madison School is at the opposite side of town from Adams School, so it isn't feasible for the bus driver to drive to both of these schools on the same day.
- Teachers A and B at Adams School prefer the 9:15 AM slot.
- Teachers B and D at Jefferson School need to have their classes back to school by 10:30 AM for gym.

Again, there can be many variations. The schedule may look like this:

	9:15 AM	10:15 AM
October 15, 2008	Jefferson B	Jefferson C
October 29, 2008	Jefferson D	Jefferson A
November 12, 2008	Washington A	Washington B
November 19, 2008	Adams A	Adams C
December 3, 2008	Adams B	Adams D
December 10, 2008	Adams E	Contingency
December 17, 2008	Madison A	Contingency
January 21, 2009	Contingency	Contingency
February 4, 2009	Contingency	Contingency

In this example, there are contingency slots worked into the schedule on December 10 and 17, since the bus driver can't travel to Adams and Madison schools on the same day. You can choose to match each of these classes with a class from another school, but if you do, make sure the bus driver knows there are two schools involved. We have seen classes stranded at either the public library or the school when the driver didn't realize who was supposed to go where and at what time. Generally, if two schools are not close together, do not try to combine their visits on a single day.

Class Size

You will need to know how many children are in each class in order to send enough library card applications and parent letters. Ask your school liaison to furnish this information on the schedule of class visit dates. With this addition, your schedule could look like this:

	9:15 AM	*10:15* AM
October 15, 2008	Jefferson B (20)	Jefferson C (18)
October 29, 2008	Jefferson D (19)	Jefferson A (20)
November 12, 2008	Washington A (22)	Washington B (22)
November 19, 2008	Adams A (23)	Adams C (24)
December 3, 2008	Adams B (22)	Adams D (21)
December 10, 2008	Adams E (23)	Contingency
December 17, 2008	Madison A (24)	Contingency
January 21, 2009	Contingency	Contingency
February 4, 2009	Contingency	Contingency

The same schedule can also be written in this format:

October 15, 2008
Jefferson School
9:15   Teacher B (20)
10:15   Teacher C (18)

October 29, 2008
Jefferson School
9:15   Teacher D (19)
10:15   Teacher A (20)

November 12, 2008
Washington School
9:15   Teacher A (22)
10:15   Teacher B (22)

November 19, 2008
Adams School
9:15   Teacher A (23)
10:15   Teacher C (24)

December 3, 2008
Adams School
9:15   Teacher B (22)
10:15   Teacher D (21)

December 10, 2008
Adams School
9:15   Teacher E (23)
10:15   Contingency

December 17, 2008
Madison School
9:15   Teacher A (24)
10:15   Contingency

January 24, 2009
Contingency

February 4, 2009
Contingency

Whichever format you prefer, make sure the schedule includes the date, school, name of teacher, and number of students for each second grade class. Once you and the school liaison have approved the dates, the liaison should distribute copies of the schedule to all the teachers and principals involved, as well as to the bus company.

Ask everyone to read it carefully to make certain the times that affect them are workable. If corrections need to be made, it is better to do so before the first bus rolls up to your door.

Of course, there is always the chance that something unexpected may come up, such as school cancellations due to bad weather or a power failure. Hopefully, the contingency dates will cover those emergencies. For other possible scenarios, please see Chapter Seven.

IDEAS FOR TEACHING BOOK RESPONSIBILITY

Library card distribution is always an important part of the class visit. At that time, we make it clear to students that with their library card comes a certain amount of responsibility. Even children who already have library cards can use a refresher course on book responsibility. Here are some methods we use to accomplish this with the younger grades (kindergarten through grade three).

Their First Charge Card

By kindergarten, most children know that a charge card is something grown-ups use to buy things and is therefore a form of currency. When we give children their library cards, we tell them that this is their very first charge card, and it is just as important as the cards their parents have. Show them that their name is on their card, along with a special barcode number that no one else in the world has. The library's computer will scan that barcode whenever the card is used to check something out and charge the item to the child's own account. The child will be held accountable for whatever happens to that item and should take this responsibility seriously.

Due Dates and Book Condition

Explain what a due date is and show the children how to tell when their book has to be returned to the library. Whether your library stamps a card inside the book, prints a receipt, or uses another method, make sure children understand the number of days your books circulate and where they can find that information. Tell them that they will be allowed to use their new library card to check out one book today, and when they return it, they can check out more books as well as other materials. They should also be made aware of the consequences they face if the book is not returned on time or comes back in poor condition.

You can illustrate this point by asking some "What if...?" questions and letting the children supply the answers. Such as:

Q: What happens if you check out a book but don't bring it back on time?
A: You will have to pay a fine of X cents per day for every book that is late.

Q: What happens if you lose the book or forget all about it and never bring it back?
A: Then you will have to pay for it so we can get a replacement.

Q: What happens if you let your dog chew it, or your baby brother scribbles on the pages with crayon, or you drop it in a mud puddle and it gets all yucky?
A: The book will be ruined and you will have to pay for it so we can buy another one. Another answer to these two questions is that if the book is lost or destroyed, no one else can check it out either—which isn't fair to other people who want to read it.

Q: What if you let someone else use your library card and that person ruins or loses the book? Who is responsible?

A: You are, since it was checked out on your card. You, not your friend, will have to give us money to purchase another copy of the book. At this point, reinforce the lesson that their library card is like a charge card and checking out a book from the library is similar to buying something from a store. The person whose name is on the card is responsible for paying back the debt or, in this case, returning the book.

Then ask the children for some ideas that can help them to remember when their book is due. Answers may include making a note on the calendar, taping the receipt on the refrigerator door, keeping all library books together in a special place so they won't get lost, etc. Acknowledge all their good ideas and tell them the exact date by which today's book must be returned. Make sure they know where to return books (to an outside book drop, at the circulation desk, etc.) If your library allows renewals, briefly explain that process.

Also explain that Anytown Public Library materials must be returned to Anytown Public Library, not to the school library. Show children where they can find the name of your library on a book and tell them to be sure to look there so they return the book to the correct place. Even if a book is returned on time, if it is brought to the wrong library, it may get lost and the child would have to pay for it.

Book Care, Part 1

If a child is old enough to attend school, he/she is old enough to learn how to properly care for a book. Book care should be an important part of every kindergarten and first grade visit, but it need not be boring.

There are several creative ways to teach book care to children. One method is to save books that have been returned in horrible condition and show them to the class. Let the children tell you what is wrong—ripped or missing pages, torn spine, pages stuck together with gum, etc. Stress the gross factor (E-yew!) and ask the children if they would treat a book like that (No!), or what they would do if they saw someone else mistreating a book (take it away from them).

To add to the fun, you can dress up like a doctor (white coat, rubber gloves, and stethoscope) and examine a sick book. Or let a child pretend to be a doctor and describe what is wrong with it. Some books may be cured or at least kept alive a little longer by taping torn pages or erasing pencil marks, but the worst cases will have to be declared dead. Tell the class that no one else will be able to enjoy those poor books that have been damaged beyond repair. Have the children promise to never, ever hurt a book like that. If you ham up this sad part, the lesson will be silly rather than depressing, and you will get your point across.

Book Care, Part 2

A song is another good way to teach a lesson to young children. You can demonstrate the proper way to treat a book and reinforce each step by leading the children in a song, "This Is the Way We Care for a Book." The following song (in italics) is sung to the tune of "Here We Go 'Round the Mulberry Bush." It is simple enough so that the children can easily learn the pattern and sing along with you.

Begin by showing the children how to pick up a book. Tell them that they shouldn't pick it up just by the front cover with the pages and back cover hanging loose, because the pages might get crumpled or the spine broken. Instead, they should carefully pick up the entire book, using two hands if necessary, keeping the book closed. If a book is in a bookcase, they shouldn't yank at the spine since it may rip, but gently wiggle the book out. Then demonstrate again while singing the first verse:

> *This is the way we take a book, take a book, take a book*
> *This is the way we take a book*
> *To show a book we love it.*

Next, demonstrate how to hold a book right side up, and sing:

> *This is the way we hold a book, hold a book, hold a book*
> *This is the way we hold a book*
> *To show a book we love it.*

Demonstrate opening a book while the book is upright and again when it is lying in your lap. Tell children that the front cover of the book should be facing the reader. Carefully, lift up the top right corner of the front cover with your right hand and open the book wide. Do not open it too much so that the front and back covers touch, since that will also break the spine of the book. Then sing:

> *This is the way we open a book, open a book, open a book*
> *This is the way we open a book*
> *To show a book we love it.*

Show how to turn one page at a time, again using your right hand and lifting the page at the top right corner. Do not grab several pages and fling them over, or scrunch the middle of the page in your fist, since that will cause it to rip. Sing:

> *This is the way we turn the page, turn the page, turn the page*
> *This is the way we turn the page*
> *To show a book we love it.*

Indicate with your finger how to read a book from left to right, and sing:

> *This is the way we read a book, read a book, read a book*
> *This is the way we read a book*
> *To show a book we love it.*

Hold up the book so the class can see the pictures and sing:

> *This is the way we share a book, share a book, share a book*
> *This is the way we share a book*
> *To show a book we love it.*

Ask the children if they should be eating cookies or a jelly sandwich while leaning over a book. When they answer no, ask them to explain why not (you might get cookie crumbs or sticky food on the pages). Ask if they should be eating an ice cream cone or drinking juice while leaning over a book. Then let them tell you why not (you might drip ice cream or spill juice onto the pages). Then sing:

> *This is the way we keep it clean, keep it clean, keep it clean*
> *This is the way we keep it clean*
> *To show a book we love it.*

Hold up assorted items, such as a pencil, a wet leaf, a piece of Swiss cheese (a felt replica will do), a worm (felt or gummy), and other inappropriate objects and ask children if any of them should be used as a bookmark. When the children answer "no," show them a paper bookmark and insert it between two pages. Then sing:

> *This is the way we mark our place, mark our place, mark our place*
> *This is the way we mark our place*
> *To show a book we love it.*

Model how to gently close a book, rather than snapping it shut. Sing:

> *This is the way we close a book, close a book, close a book*
> *This is the way we close a book*
> *To show a book we love it.*

Ask children how they should put a book down. Should they throw it on the floor? Fling it across the room? Place it on the edge of a table where it is sure to fall down? Stick it on top of a pile of dirty dishes? When they reply "no," show them how to gently place the book down on a clean, solid surface, and sing:

> *This is the way we put it down, put it down, put it down*
> *This is the way we put it down*
> *To show a book we love it.*

Now discuss where to store a book. On a messy table? In the dirty laundry basket? In the sandbox? Under the kitchen sink? Think up a few more ridiculous places and let the children call out "no" to each one. Then show them how to neatly place the book on a book shelf. Remind them that the shelf should be tall enough to fit the book without scraping and not so tight that you have to jam it in. Then sing:

> *This is the way we store a book, store a book, store a book*
> *This is the way we store a book*
> *To show a book we love it.*

Finally, ask the children to review the correct way to treat a book, quickly recapping the main point of each verse. Then end with:

> *This is the way we care for a book, care for a book, care for a book*
> *This is the way we care for a book*
> *To show a book we love it.*

Book Care Part 3

Puppets are popular during story time and can also be used to demonstrate book care. When you sit down to read a story to the class, introduce your puppet friend. Use whatever puppet is most comfortable to you, but it should be one that you can operate using one hand. It should have either arms that move or a mouth that opens and closes so you can have it pick up things and grab hold of your book. The most important thing is that your puppet should have a mischievous personality.

Introduce your puppet to the class. Allow your puppet to say hello to the children and establish it as a loveable but naughty little scoundrel that you have to scold often. The puppet should get very excited when you tell the children that you are about to read a book. It won't quiet down until you agree to let it help you. Select a book that is not too wordy and that has something to do with reading or libraries.

When you show the book to the class, your puppet should jump up and try to grab the book from your other hand. ("That's my all-time favorite book!") You will have to say that books should not be used for playing tug-of-war. Your puppet will want to do everything—turn the pages, read the story, point out all the pictures, etc., and you will have to tell it to calm down or you will not continue. (Hopefully, any antsy children in the group will also take the hint.) Insist on reading the story yourself, but your puppet can help by turning the pages and discussing the story with you.

As you read the book, your puppet will exhibit some of the undesirable behaviors demonstrated in the previous lesson. It will hold the book upside down, be rough when turning the pages, try to eat while leaning over the book, drop a worm onto the pages, etc. Each time the puppet does something wrong, ask the class if that is the proper way to treat a book. Then have the children explain to your puppet how it should behave. You can also ask them to tell your puppet the proper way to act while someone is reading to the class. When you finish the book, your puppet will try to throw it on the floor. Again, you and the students will have to admonish it. By the end of the presentation, your puppet and students should have learned the proper way to care for a book.

If you have time, you can do a follow-up activity to reinforce the lesson on book responsibility. (See appendix D for activity sheets.)

IDEAS FOR TEACHING CALL NUMBERS

In the course of having done many school visits over the years, we have discovered a number of ideas that work well with school groups. If the class is divided into two groups, one group will start with the tour of the department while the other group starts with the online catalog demonstration. Following are methods we have found helpful when introducing call numbers and collection codes to both groups. Of course, if the call numbers or collection codes are assigned differently in your library, adapt this lesson as necessary.

During the Tour

These suggestions work especially well with second and third grade classes. If older students already understand the concept of a call number, skip the "address" explanation.

Tell students to imagine that the Children's Department is a town, and the various collection areas are neighborhoods in the town. Each row of shelves is a street, and each book is a house on the street. Ask children to tell you how they find a particular house on a street. Someone will answer, "by the address." Tell them it is the same way with books. Each book has an address, also known as a call number or Dewey decimal number. This address is written on a label that is stuck onto the spine of the book. When you look up this book in the online catalog, it will tell you this same call number.

Next explain that each neighborhood, or collection area, has a special code which is part of the call number (address) and also appears on the spine label. For example, the code for picture books is "PJ." Point to the shelves where the picture books are located and show that the end panels of the bookcases have "PJ" on them. Then pull out a picture book and show them that the spine label also starts with PJ.

Ask them to tell you what is written below PJ on the spine label, and the children will read the letters that appear there. Explain how these are the first letters of the author's last name (in some libraries, it may be the entire name) and show them the author's name on the book cover. Ask a child what his/her last name is and have him/her tell you how his/her name would appear on the spine label of a book. Say it is very important to know the author's last name because all fiction books are shelved in alphabetical (ABC) order by the author's last name. Then go over the terms "fiction" and "nonfiction," "author" and "illustrator." Point out where the last names beginning with "A" start, and how the books go in order up and down the rows until they end with the "Z" names.

It's a good idea to pull out a few picture books from different shelves and show children how the spine labels all start with PJ and that the next few letters match the first letters of the author's last name, even if the illustrator is more famous! Warn them that they need to remember this, because you will be quizzing them later. (Which you should do, as you move to the easy reader and juvenile fiction collections.)

As you go to the various collection areas, have the students repeat the collection codes and point to each area you have visited so far: PJ for picture books, E for easy readers, J for hardcover fiction, JPB for paperback fiction, etc. Substitute your library's collection codes if they differ from these. (Children usually want to know why many of the call numbers have a J. We explain that "J" stands for "juvenile" which is a fancy word for children.) This repetition helps the children to remember these areas. Later, when you do the online catalog demonstration, point out these collection codes when they appear on the screen and have the students tell you what they mean and where the materials are located.

As you move to the nonfiction area, explain that these books are not shelved by the author's last name, but by subject, and that each subject has a different number as part of its code. It is helpful to have bookmarks listing some of the more popular subjects and their call number prefixes posted on the end panels of the nonfiction shelves, so the children can see what you mean. Tell them that fiction books have only letters in their call numbers, but nonfiction books will have both letters and numbers. In our library, the Children's nonfiction books start with J followed by some numbers, the Young Adult nonfiction starts with YA, and the Adult nonfiction has no letters in front of the number. Let children know how books are labeled in your library. Then, when they see a nonfiction number on the computer screen, they will be able to tell if it is a children's book or not by how the call number begins.

When you come to the biography section, ask them first if they know what a biography is. Most children will not, but some may notice that there are numbers mixed in with letters, indicating the books are nonfiction. When you show them a book about someone whose name they recognize, they will figure out that a biography is a true book about a real person, who either lived a long time ago or is alive today.

As you go from circulating books to media, tell them how long these items can be checked out. For example, videos and DVDs may have a shorter circulation time than books. Also review why it is important for them to return their materials on time and in good condition. At the reference collection, show them different types of reference books and tell children that these items must be used in the library and cannot be checked out.

Throughout the tour, allow the children to interact by letting them read the spine labels. Play a game with the various collection codes by quizzing the children often. (What is a PJ? A picture book!) What does the Se stand for? Seuss! How do you know J932 is nonfiction? It has numbers!) This repetition will reinforce learning.

After the tour, you can give children time to browse for a book. Now that they are familiar with the various collection areas, they will know where to go to find the type of book they want.

During the Online Catalog Demonstration

Since children will see call numbers on the screen as they look up books, you should make sure they are familiar with the various collection codes in use. An easy way to do this is to do a show-and-tell using flash cards and books that exemplify these collections.

Before the class visits begin, you should create a set of flash cards printed with the collection codes you will be teaching. Make more cards with the titles of the book(s) you will be looking up and the author(s). Print the author cards exactly as you want the students to enter them in the computer, that is, with the author's last name before the first name. Tell them that you look up an author by the last name, then first name. This is because that is how the fiction books are arranged on the shelves. You can also make cards for other terms, such as "fiction," "nonfiction," "keyword," "subject," and other words you may use during the online demonstration. Have the books you will be using ready on a nearby table or cart.

Children who are sitting at the computers are not going to endure a long teacher-like lesson, so you need to be very upbeat, interactive, and quick. You can use the "street address" explanation mentioned previously, and hold up each flash card with the corresponding book. Orally quiz students by holding up the flash cards and letting them call out and point to each collection area. Have children tell you how they would type their names (last name, first name) to do an author search in the computer. Once you have established the difference between fiction on nonfiction, hold up a book and let a child read the spine label, tell you the name of the collection, and point to the location. Make it a game, and this instruction will be fun. Don't try to explain the different nonfiction subject prefixes at this point. You can point them out later on during the tour.

As you search for books on the computer, point out the various call numbers that are listed on the screen. Ask the children to tell you if each item is a book or not, located in the Children's Department or not, fiction or nonfiction. Have them explain how they figured that out just by looking at the call number. They will be amazed to realize how much they already know without actually seeing the book. We tell our students that once they understand the secret code (our collection prefixes) they can almost always track down what they are looking for on their own, just like a detective!

Later, when you walk them through the department, take the flash cards with you and hold them up to the signs on the bookshelves to further reinforce what they learned. This tour should go faster than the other group's since you already covered much of the information while at the computers.

If you have time, you can do a follow-up activity to help children remember call numbers and collection codes. (See appendix D for activity sheets.)

SAMPLE STAFF LISTS

An elementary school class visit will affect the staffing needs of other departments besides Youth Services. Some of the general factors to be considered are:

- Is there a direct entrance to the Children's Department from the outside?
- Will there be more than one class visiting on a given day?
- What time will the first class arrive and will it be before the library opens to the public?
- Will students be allowed to check out books? Will they check out books themselves or will a page take care of checking them out?
- Are children's books checked out in the Children's Department or in another area?
- Does your library have a computer lab and/or program area that is separate from your book collection?
- What grade level is the class and what elements will you include in the visit?
- Into how many groups will the class be divided?
- Will there be other children's programs, such as story time, going on at the time of the class visit?
- Do you plan to present a skit or other activity that requires more than one person?

The following exercises present a variety of factors to help you plan the number of building-wide library staff required for a class visit.

Assumptions for a Kindergarten Class Visit:

- One kindergarten class will visit.
- The class will arrive at 9:15 AM, before the library opens at 10:00 AM.
- The visit will take 45 minutes.
- The Children's Department is on the second floor, with no separate entrance from outside.
- The visit will consist of a short skit about book care, a story, distribution of library cards, time for children to select a book, and a craft.
- The class of 20 children will stay together for the skit and story, then be divided into two groups for library card distribution, book selection and the craft. Each group will have at least one parent chaperone, not including the teacher.
- The program and craft areas are adjacent to the Children's book collection.
- Books are checked out at the circulation desk in the lobby, not in the Children's Department, and a page will take care of this.

- There will not be any other programs going on at the time of the visit.
- The skit requires two people.

For a Kindergarten Class Visit, You Will Need at Least

- **One** custodian or other person responsible for opening the building, turning on lights, etc.
- **One** person at Circulation to check out books and process last minute applications
- **Two** Children's librarians to present the skit and lead the two groups (one of whom will greet class as they arrive and take them upstairs)
- **One** page or other support staff to help set up materials, bring children's book selections to Circulation to check out, take teacher evaluation forms, and generally troubleshoot

Assumptions for a Second Grade Class Visit:

- Two second grade classes will visit.
- The first class will arrive at 9:15 AM, before the library opens at 10:00 AM.
- The visit will take one hour.
- The second class will arrive at 10:15 AM, as the first class is leaving.
- The Children's Department is on the second floor, with no separate entrance from outside.
- The visit will consist of a tour of the Children's Department, distribution of library cards, time for children to select a book, a story, and a simple search on the online catalog.
- Once they arrive in the Children's Department, each class of 20 students will be divided into two groups, and each group will have at least one parent chaperone, not including the teacher.
- The program room is adjacent to the book collection.
- The online catalog instruction will take place in the computer lab, which has ten patron computers and is staffed separately.
- Books are checked out at the circulation desk in the lobby, not in the Children's Department, and a page will take care of this.
- There will not be any other programs going on at the time of the visit, but other patrons will be able to use the Children's Department when the library opens at 10 AM.

For a Second Grade Class Visit, You Will Need at Least:

- **One** custodian or other person responsible for opening the building, turning on lights, etc.

- **One** person at Circulation to check out books and process last minute applications

- **Two** Children's librarians to lead two groups (one of whom will greet class as they arrive and take them upstairs)

- **One** additional Children's librarian arriving before the library opens at 10:00 AM to assist other patrons. This librarian can also greet the 10:15 AM class in the lobby if they arrive before the first class has finished.

- **One** page or other support staff to help set up materials, bring children's book selections to Circulation to check out, take teacher evaluation forms, and generally troubleshoot

- **One** librarian or technician to staff the computer lab and help with instruction

Assumptions for a Fifth Grade Class Visit:

- One fifth grade class will visit for the purpose of beginning research on a new assignment.

- The class will arrive at 10:00 AM, after the library opens at 9:30 AM.

- The visit will take one hour and 15 minutes.

- The Children's Department is on the lower level of the building and has a separate entrance from the outside.

- The visit will consist of the distribution of library cards, a discussion of the general resources available in the Children's Department, a preview of reference and circulating materials that pertain to the class project, a demonstration on how to search the online catalog for more materials, instruction on how to find additional information on selected computer databases, time for students to take notes and select materials, time to check out materials.

- The class of 20 students will be divided into two groups, and each group will have at least one parent chaperone, not including the teacher.

- A cart of reference and circulating books and media materials pertaining to this assignment has been set aside for this class.

- The online catalog and database instruction will take place in the computer lab, which has ten patron computers and is staffed separately.

- Books are checked out in the Children's Department by the students.

- There will not be any other programs going on at the time of the visit, but other patrons are likely to be using the area since the library is open.

For a Fifth Grade Class Visit, You Will Need at Least:

- **One** Children's librarian to introduce students to the reference and circulating materials

- **One** Librarian or Technician to demonstrate the online resources in the computer lab
- **One** Children's librarian to help walk-in patrons. This librarian can also assist with the class visit as needed and check out materials at the Children's desk.
- **One** Page or other support staff to help set up materials, shuttle the groups back and forth to the computer lab, take teacher evaluation forms, and generally troubleshoot

If you have a key and can open the outside entrance to the Children's Department, you may not require a custodian, even if the class is scheduled to arrive at 9:15 AM. And since books are checked out in the department, you would not need a staff member at the circulation desk to help with your visitors.

These lists are bare bones requirements and do not consider staff needed to operate the rest of the library.

TIMELINE FOR CLASS VISIT PREPARATION

While the school liaison is scheduling the elementary school visits:

- Prepare templates for letters to teachers, parents, and principals
- Prepare teacher evaluation forms
- Prepare any activity sheets you will use with children during the visit and/or to give teachers to use with the class after they return to school
- Develop any brochures, book lists, or other materials you want to give to teachers
- Obtain envelopes for teacher letters, folders for teacher packets, and library card applications
- Determine exactly what you will cover during the visit, how it will be done, and who will do it
- Make a schedule of what will happen on the day of the visit, indicating the time each part should occur
- Design any maps, games, or other instructional materials to use during the visit and order bookmarks to give to students

When you receive the schedule from your school liaison:

- Verify the teachers' names and the number of students in each class on the schedule
- Check the dates against your calendar to make sure they are workable
- Inform other departments of the class visit schedule and make sure there are no conflicts
- Notify the school liaison of any conflicts ASAP and reschedule dates if needed
- Assign staff to do visits; modify routines as needed
- Pull books that will be read and used for the online catalog demonstration; check them out to the department (if using the same books for all class visits)
- Have staff members rehearse their talks, skits, and online demonstrations
- Reserve the computer lab for class visit dates (if applicable).

Three to four weeks prior to each visit:

- Print materials as needed
- Assemble and mail pre-visit packets to teachers and letters to principals

One week prior to each visit:

- Check for the return of library card applications; call the teacher if needed
- Prepare new library cards; call teacher or parents if there are problems
- Prepare craft materials and count out bookmarks to give class
- Assemble post-visit packet materials for the teacher

Two days prior to each visit:

- Call the teacher to remind him/her about the upcoming visit
- Make sure the library cards are done and in the department

One day prior to each visit:

- Place evaluation forms on clipboards with pencils
- Remind the custodian, Circulation staff, and other staff of the next day's visit
- Place class visit materials, post-visit folders, etc. where readily accessible
- Reserve a book cart on which students will place their selections
- Make sure all computers are working and test online searches

The day of each visit:

- Arrive at least 15 minutes before the class is due
- Set up areas and materials
- Turn on and test computers
- Check to make sure a Circulation clerk and other people outside of your department who are involved with the class visit have arrived
- Station one person at the designated entrance to greet the class
- **CONDUCT THE CLASS VISIT!**

Immediately after each visit:

- Return areas to normal and put away materials
- Thank staff verbally for their efforts, especially those outside your department
- Read evaluations and save for later

After all class visits are completed:

- Read evaluations and compile data
- Meet with department members to discuss what worked and what needs to be changed
- Thank staff in other departments for their cooperation
- Report class visit statistics and teacher evaluation summary to library director
- Contact the school liaison to share feedback and discuss what worked and what needs to be changed
- Resume your "normal" schedule!

ANYTOWN PUBLIC LIBRARY
CHILD LIBRARY CARD APPLICATION

PLEASE PRINT LEGIBLY   Date _____

Child's Last Name   First Name   Initial

Child's Address: Street

City   State   Zip Code

Phone Number   Child's Date of Birth: Month/Date/Year

Signature of Applicant (Child)

❏ Check here to limit your child to Children's materials only

I agree to obey the rules of Anytown Public Library and to be responsible for all materials charged to my child's card. I agree to be responsible for all fees my child incurs for any overdue, lost, or damaged materials. In the event my child's card is lost or stolen, I will notify the library. Replacement charge for a lost card is $1.00.

Parent/Guardian Name

Parent/Guardian Signature

Email address (If you want to receive overdue/hold notices via email)

ANYTOWN PUBLIC LIBRARY
CHILD LIBRARY CARD APPLICATION

PLEASE PRINT LEGIBLY   Date _____

Child's Last Name   First Name   Initial

Child's Address: Street

City   State   Zip Code

Phone Number   Child's Date of Birth: Month/Date/Year

Signature of Applicant (Child)

❏ Check here to limit your child to Children's materials only

I agree to obey the rules of Anytown Public Library and to be responsible for all materials charged to my child's card. I agree to be responsible for all fees my child incurs for any overdue, lost, or damaged materials. In the event my child's card is lost or stolen, I will notify the library. Replacement charge for a lost card is $1.00.

Parent/Guardian Name

Parent/Guardian Signature

Email address (If you want to receive overdue/hold notices via email)

PARENT LETTER

[your library header here]

Today's Date

Dear Parent/Guardian,

Your child's second grade class will be visiting the Anytown Public Library on day of the week, month, day, year. The children will take a tour of the Children's Department, listen to a story, and learn how to look up a book using our online catalog. Each child will also be allowed to check out one book.

In order for your child to take out a book, he/she must have a valid Anytown Public Library card. If your child already owns a library card, please make sure he/she brings it on the day of the class visit. If your child does not have a library card, please complete the enclosed application and return it to your child's teacher as soon as possible, so the card will be ready on the date of your child's visit.

Before filling out the library card application for your child, please read the following instructions. Remember that the information should pertain to your second grade child, and not another member of your household. Please print legibly so that we can read the information correctly. We appreciate your cooperation.

1. Print your **child's** last name, first name, and middle initial on the line provided
2. Print your **child's** address and date of birth where indicated
3. Have your **child** sign on the line labeled "Signature of Applicant"
4. Print your name on the line for "Parent/Guardian Name" and sign your name below

We hope that your child enjoys using his/her library card to check out a book during the scheduled school visit. Children's books can be checked out for three weeks and then must be returned to the library. A fine of 10 cents per day will accumulate until an overdue book is returned. If a book is lost, you are responsible for the cost of replacing the book plus any additional fees incurred. Please note that any books borrowed by your child from Anytown Public Library must be returned directly to the library, not to the school. The school is not responsible for returning materials that are checked out during class visits. Thank you very much for your cooperation.

We are happy to answer any questions you have about library cards or your child's visit. Please call us at: (000) 000–0000 if:

- You do not know if your child has a library card
- Your child has a card from another town library
- Your child has fines on his/her library card
- You want to inform us of any special circumstances regarding your child
- You have any other concerns

We have asked that the teachers bring some parent chaperones to assist during the class visit. Please let your child's teacher know if you would like to come to the library with the class.

We look forward to seeing your child at Anytown Public Library.

> Sincerely,
> Your Name, Children's Librarian

Note: Substitute your own information throughout the letter. You may want to add other information about overdue fines, library hours, or special programs for children of this age group. Other issues you may want to address in the parent letter may include what to do if the child does not live in the same city as the library and how to limit the child to checking out only materials from the Children's Department.

PRINCIPAL LETTER

[your library header here]

Principal
Elementary School
Street
Anytown, State, 00000

Today's Date

Dear Principal,

On date of first visit, we will begin conducting our annual tours of the Children's Department for all Anyschool second grade students and their teachers. We are committed to helping your students achieve the best possible education, and we thank you for supporting this collaboration between the schools and the public library.

Each second grade class will spend an hour at the library. During this time, we will take the children on a short tour of the Children's Department, distribute library cards, read them a story, and show them how to search for a book using our online catalog. Each child will be allowed to check out one book. We will ask the teachers to fill out a short evaluation form to let us know how we are doing and how we can best meet their needs in the future. We will also give the teachers activity sheets so they can follow up on the visit with their class after they return to school. Attached are copies of the letters we are sending to the teachers and parents concerning the class visits.

Thank you for allowing us to continue these valuable library orientation sessions with your classes. If you have any concerns, please do not hesitate to contact us. We look forward to working with you for another successful school year.

Sincerely,
Your Name, Children's Librarian

Note: This letter can be adapted to send to the school superintendent or other school or town official. Substitute your own information as needed.

TEACHER LETTER

[your library header here]

Teacher
Elementary School
Street
Anytown, State, 00000

Today's Date

Dear Teacher,

We have arranged with Ms. School Liaison and Ms. Principal to invite all the second grade classes in Anyschool to tour the Children's Department at Anytown Public Library this school year. We are delighted to welcome your students to our library on day of the week, month, day, year. A school bus will pick up your class at the school and bring you to Anytown Library. We will have someone waiting to greet you at the library's parking lot entrance at 9:15 AM. The bus will pick up your class to return you to school at 10:15 AM.

During your class's visit to the library, we will be taking them on a short tour of the Children's Department, distributing library cards to students who turned in application forms, reading a story, and showing the students how to search for a book using our online catalog. Each child will be allowed to check out one book.

We would like your class to have an enjoyable and productive visit. In order to facilitate this, we request that you help us by doing the following:

1. Arrange to have two or more chaperones accompany your class, since the children will be divided into two groups during the visit.

2. The teacher and chaperones should remain with their assigned group for the duration of the visit and assist their students as necessary.

3. Have each child wear a name tag so that we may call on them by name. It helps to color code the name tags so the children and library staff will know which group they are in.

4. Notify us in advance if any of your students requires special assistance or if you have any unusual circumstances.

Since the children will be checking out books, it is important that each child bring a valid library card, if they have one. Children who do not have a library card should be given a library card application to take home to have a parent complete. Some application forms are enclosed, and you may make more copies if needed. We would appreciate your assistance in making sure the forms are filled out correctly and returned to the library in a timely matter. Please check the completed forms to make sure that:

1. The child's last name, first name, and middle initial are printed legibly at the top of the application.

2. The child's correct address, phone number, and date of birth are given.

3. The child's signature (not the parent's) appears on the space provided for "Signature of Applicant."

4. The parent/guardian's signature appears on the proper line, with the name printed legibly below.

Please distribute the library card applications to your students immediately and request that parents/guardians complete the applications and return them to you as soon as possible. Each child should also take home one of the enclosed parent letters which explains the purpose of this visit.

Please return the library card applications batched together with your name and the school's name clearly written on the top left corner of the envelope, along with the scheduled date of your visit. We prefer that you bring them in to our Circulation Department in person, to assure that the forms arrive safely. If that is not possible, please send them via the mail. We must receive the applications at least one week before the class visit date in order to process them in time.

Thank you for your cooperation. Please call us if you have any questions or special requirements. We look forward to meeting you and your students!

Sincerely,
Your Name, Children's Librarian

Note: Substitute your own information throughout the letter as needed. You may want to include additional information in your letter, such as:

- Any other information that is required on the library card application
- Instructions for permission forms for the class trip
- What to do if a child has fines on his/her library card
- What to do if a child is from out of town and is not able to obtain a card from your library
- Your library's policy for overdue books
- Information about the Teacher Loan Card
- Information about the evaluation form that you will ask teachers to complete on class visit day
- The name of the library building where the visit will occur and the address if your public library has more than one branch.
- Asking the teacher to inform you of any children who do not speak English, what language they do speak, and the child's country of origin if possible. This is so you can prepare appropriate materials for the child.
- Asking that a parent or aid accompany children with special needs.

TEACHER/CHAPERONE EVALUATION FORM

(*Note:* Customize as needed to reflect the elements included in your presentation. The form should take up one side of a letter-size sheet of paper.)

[your library header here]

School: _____   Date: _____

Your name: _____

This form is filled out by a (check one):

❏ Teacher   ❏ Media Specialist   ❏ Parent Chaperone   ❏ Other

1. Did you find this visit helpful to your students?

❏ Yes, very helpful   ❏ Somewhat helpful   ❏ Not helpful

2. Was the overall presentation well organized?

❏ Yes, very organized   ❏ Somewhat organized   ❏ Not organized

3. Was the library staff knowledgeable?

❏ Yes, very knowledgeable   ❏ Somewhat knowledgeable   ❏ Not knowledgeable

4. Rank in order of importance (1= most important, 4= least important).

___ Tour of the Children's Department   ___ Story time
___ Library card distribution   ___ Online catalog instruction
___ Craft   ___ Book care skit

5. About how often to you visit Anytown Public Library? _____

6. Do you have an Anytown Public Library teacher loan card?

❏ Yes   ❏ No

7. Would you like us to add or cut anything from the class visit?

_____

8. Please write any additional comments on the back.

TEACHER FOLLOW-UP LETTER

[your library header here]

Today's Date

Dear Teacher,

We hope you and your students enjoyed your field trip to the Anytown Public Library. It is always a pleasure to introduce children to the library and its resources. We hope that you and your students will make a habit of frequenting the Children's Department for help with school assignments and for recreational reading.

You have received a bag containing the books your students checked out. Each book will have the student's library card inside the front cover. Please note the date these books are due and remind your students to return their books directly to Anytown Public Library, not to the school. Perhaps you can post the due date on your bulletin board to make it easier for them to remember. Let them know that they are responsible for returning the books on time and in good condition and that fines will be charged for books that are overdue, damaged, or lost. Also tell your students that they will be able to check out other books and media from Anytown Public Library after this book is returned. If a child needs more time with a book, he/she may renew it by calling the circulation desk at (000) 000–0000. Books may also be renewed on the library's Web site.

Also included in the bag are bookmarks for your students and some activity sheets to help you follow-up on the lessons presented during the class visit. You may make additional copies if needed. In addition, we have enclosed an Assignment Alert Form, which you can copy and use to inform us of upcoming assignments. Forms may be returned by mail or fax, or submitted online via our web site. Please feel free to contact us by phone or email or to come by the library if you would like us to gather materials for your class.

Thank you for sharing your class time with us. We look forward to serving you and your students.

Sincerely,
Your Name, Children's Librarian

Note: Substitute your own information as needed and customize other sections to reflect your class visit.

APPENDIX D

Elementary School Student Activity Sheets

Bookmarks to Color
Library Scavenger Hunt: Grades 2–6
Matching Activity Sheet: Grades 2–3
Matching Activity Sheet: Grades 3–5
Matching Activity Sheet: Grades 5–6
Library Terms Word Search Puzzle
Library Terms Crossword Puzzle
Collection Areas Word Search Puzzle
Collection Areas Crossword Puzzle
Post-Visit Activity Sheet: Kindergarten and Grade 1
Post-Visit Activity Sheet: Grades 2–3
Post-Visit Activity Sheet: Grades 4–6
Children's Department Bookmarks

ELEMENTARY SCHOOL STUDENT ACTIVITY SHEETS

The following pages contain several activity sheets that you can give children to do during a class visit to reinforce some of the library facts they learned. These can also be given to the teacher to take back to the classroom. Feel free to adapt any of these to match your own needs and library collections. You may also choose to shorten or expand some of the activities. Answer sheets are provided as applicable.

BOOKMARKS TO COLOR

Stamping Bookmarks:

Provide construction paper cut into bookmark-size strips, rubber stamps with pictures of book characters, and ink pads. Let children stamp the paper and design their own bookmarks. They can also punch a hole at the top of the bookmark and tie on a ribbon.

Bookworm Bookmarks:

Make copies of this bookworm design. Children can color in the worm to use as a bookmark

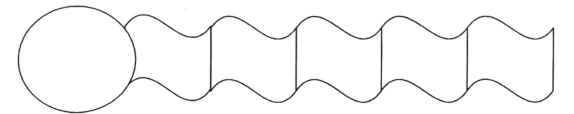

LIBRARY SCAVENGER HUNT: GRADES 2–6

(*Note:* You can let children search for items where they are normally kept or you may want to pull out a few items and put them in a contained area so children don't wreck your shelves. If you have one group doing the scavenger hunt and another group busy with another part of the program, make sure the hunters will not disturb the other students. Customize this list to suit your collection. For grades two and three, keep it simple by listing fewer types of books and having children write down just the titles. For older grades, you can tell them to write the name of the authors and/or the call numbers of the books they choose.)

DIRECTIONS: There are several types of materials listed below. Find one example of each item and write the titles on the lines provided.

1. Picture book: _____

2. Magazine: _____

3. Nonfiction book about an animal: _____

4. Biography: _____

5. Video: _____

6. Book on tape: _____

7. Board book: _____

8. Hardcover fiction book: _____

9. Easy reader: _____

10. Craft or drawing book: _____

11. Reference book: _____

12. DVD: _____

13. CD-ROM (software): _____

14. Book in a language other than English: _____

15. Nonfiction book about a country: _____

16. Paperback fiction book: _____

17. Book on CD: _____

18. Book and CD set: _____

MATCHING ACTIVITY SHEET: GRADES 2–3

During today's tour of the Children's Department, the librarian mentioned several terms that refer to various people, places, and materials you can find in the library. In the lists below, draw a line from each term to its description.
(*Note:* Customize your activity sheet to include as many of these items as you want.)

TERMS:

1. Fiction books
2. Nonfiction books
3. Picture books
4. Easy readers
5. Reference books
6. Spine label
7. Call number
8. Online catalog
9. Library card
10. Due date
11. Fine
12. Circulation desk
13. Librarian
14. Author
15. Illustrator
16. Media
17. Collection
18. Internet
19. Word processor
20. Program room

DESCRIPTIONS:

a. What you use to check out a book
b. A person who draws the pictures for a book
c. A code that helps you find the item you want
d. What you have to pay if you do not return your items in time
e. Videos, DVDs, audiobooks, music CDs, and software
f. A computer program for typing documents
g. Books with many illustrations
h. A person who writes a book
i. Books with true facts
j. What you use to look up a book or other materials
k. Books for children who are learning to read on their own
l. The place where story times are held
m. Books with made-up stories
n. Books to help with homework that do not leave the library
o. A group of similar materials
p. Where you go to check out books and other materials
q. A sticker on a book to help you find it
r. Ask this person to help you find a book or other materials
s. The date your materials must be returned by
t. An online resource you can search for information on many topics

ANSWER SHEET

Matching Activity Sheet: Grades 2–3

During today's tour of the Children's Department, the librarian mentioned several terms that refer to various people, places, and materials you can find in the library. In the lists below, draw a line from each term to its description.
(*Note:* Customize your activity sheet to include as many of these items as you want.)

TERMS:	DESCRIPTIONS:	ANSWERS:
1. Fiction books	a. What you use to check out a book	1–m
2. Nonfiction books	b. A person who draws the pictures for a book	2–i
3. Picture books	c. A code that helps you find the item you want	3–g
4. Easy readers	d. What you have to pay if you do not return your items in time	4–k
5. Reference books	e. Videos, DVDs, audiobooks, music CDs, and software	5–n
6. Spine label	f. A computer program for typing documents	6–q
7. Call number	g. Books with many illustrations	7–c
8. Online catalog	h. A person who writes a book	8–j
9. Library card	i. Books with true facts	9–a
10. Due date	j. What you use to look up a book or other materials	10–s
11. Fine	k. Books for children who are learning to read on their own	11–d
12. Circulation desk	l. The place where story times are held	12–p
13. Librarian	m. Books with made-up stories	13–r
14. Author	n. Books to help with homework that do not leave the library	14–h
15. Illustrator	o. A group of similar materials	15–b
16. Media	p. Where you go to check out books and other materials	16–e
17. Collection	q. A sticker on a book to help you find it	17–o
18. Internet	r. Ask this person to help you find a book or other materials	18–t
19. Word processor	s. The date your materials must be returned by	19–f
20. Program room	t. An online resource you can search for information on many topics	20–l

MATCHING ACTIVITY SHEET: GRADES 3–5

The Children's Department has several collection areas. In the lists below, match each collection code to the type of materials that are shelved there. Then, on the map provided, label each area in the department. (Note: Your collection codes may differ. Alter them as necessary and provide whatever area labels needed for your map.)

COLLECTION CODE:	TYPE OF MATERIALS:
1. BD	a. Nonfiction books
2. PJ	b. Software
3. E	c. Videos
4. J	d. Book and tape set
5. JPB	e. Music CDs
6. JR	f. Books on tape
7. JB	g. Easy or beginning readers
8. J 000.000	h. Paperback chapter books
9. JVC	i. Board books
10. JDVD	j. Hardcover chapter books
11. J CASSETTE FICTION	k. Books on CD
12. J CD FICTION	l. Movies on DVD
13. J CD MUSIC	m. Biographies
14. JCD-ROM	n. Reference books
15. J SET	o. Picture books

MAP OF YOUR CHILDREN'S ROOM
WITH DEFINED AREAS TO LABEL

(You may also want to include areas such as the information desk, program room, craft corner, computer lab, etc.)

ANSWER SHEET

Matching Activity Sheet: Grades 3–5

The Children's Department has several collection areas. In the lists below, match each Collection Code to the type of materials that are shelved there. Then, on the map provided, label each area in the department. (*Note:* Your collection codes may differ. Alter them as necessary and provide whatever area labels are needed for your map.)

COLLECTION CODE:	TYPE OF MATERIALS:	ANSWERS:
1. BD	a. Nonfiction books	1–i
2. PJ	b. Software	2–o
3. E	c. Videos	3–g
4. J	d. Picture books	4–j
5. JPB	e. Music CDs	5–h
6. JR	f. Books on tape (audiobooks)	6–n
7. JB	g. Reference books	7–m
8. J 000.000	h. Easy or beginning books	8–a
9. JVC	i. Paperback chapter books	9–c
10. JDVD	j. Board books	10–l
11. J CASSETTE FICTION	k. Hardcover chapter books	11–f
12. J CD FICTION	l. Movies on DVD	12–k
13. J CD MUSIC	m. Biographies	13–e
14. JCD-ROM	n. Reference books	14–b
15. J SET	o. Picture books	15–d

MAP OF YOUR CHILDREN'S ROOM
WITH DEFINED AREAS TO LABEL

(You may also want to include areas such as the information desk, program room, craft corner, computer lab, etc.)

MATCHING ACTIVITY SHEET: GRADES 5–6

All materials in the library are identified by a Dewey decimal number, also known as a call number. For nonfiction books, each number represents a specific subject area. In the lists below, match the call numbers to the corresponding subject areas. (*Note:* Your call numbers may be different. Alter as needed.)

CALL NUMBER:	SUBJECT AREA:
1. 636.7	a. Dinosaurs
2. 932	b. Countries—Mexico
3. 641.5	c. Greek Mythology
4. 394.2	d. Sports—Football
5. 398.8	e. Biographies
6. 974.9	f. Planets—Solar System
7. 745.5	g. Fairy Tales
8. 783	h. Weather—Hurricanes
9. 292	i. Mother Goose Rhymes
10. 567	j. Ancient Egypt
11. 796.3	k. UFOs
12. 296.4	l. Cookbooks
13. 423	m. United States—New Jersey
14. 920	n. Religion—Judaism
15. 811	o. Sharks
16. 972	p. Trains
17. 001.9	q. Music—Christmas Carols
18. 398.2	r. Pets—Dogs
19. 597.3	s. Holidays—Kwanzaa
20. 523	t. Craft Books
21. 629.4	u. English Dictionary
22. 625	v. Poetry
23. 551.5	w. Astronauts

ANSWERS

Matching Activity Sheet: Grades 5–6

All materials in the library are identified by a Dewey decimal number, also known as a call number. For nonfiction books, each number represents a specific subject area. In the lists below, match the call numbers to the corresponding subject areas. (*Note:* Your call numbers may be different. Alter as needed.)

CALL NUMBER:	SUBJECT AREA:	ANSWERS:
1. 636.7	a. Dinosaurs	1–r
2. 932	b. Countries—Mexico	2–j
3. 641.5	c. Greek Mythology	3–l
4. 394.2	d. Sports—Football	4–s
5. 398.8	e. Biographies	5–i
6. 974.9	f. Planets—Solar System	6–m
7. 745.5	g. Fairy Tales	7–t
8. 783	h. Weather—Hurricanes	8–q
9. 292	i. Mother Goose Rhymes	9–c
10. 567	j. Ancient Egypt	10–a
11. 796.3	k. UFOs	11–d
12. 296.4	l. Cookbooks	12–n
13. 423	m. United States—New Jersey	13–u
14. 920	n. Religion—Judaism	14–e
15. 811	o. Sharks	15–v
16. 972	p. Trains	16–b
17. 001.9	q. Music—Christmas Carols	17–k
18. 398.2	r. Pets—Dogs	18–g
19. 597.3	s. Holidays—Kwanzaa	19–o
20. 523	t. Craft Books	20–f
21. 629.4	u. English Dictionary	21–w
22. 625	v. Poetry	22–p
23. 551.5	w. Astronauts	23–h

LIBRARY TERMS WORD SEARCH PUZZLE

C	W	D	J	L	P	Z	F	I	N	E	B	U	J	S	E	E	L
A	K	E	H	S	O	P	I	G	C	N	P	T	F	R	A	H	K
L	I	B	R	A	R	Y	C	A	R	D	C	Y	C	A	D	D	L
L	P	Q	U	S	A	R	T	M	I	N	R	T	O	O	D	U	P
N	O	N	F	I	C	T	I	O	N	N	O	V	M	T	U	R	A
U	Z	R	L	L	H	U	O	U	M	S	L	A	P	B	E	L	L
M	T	U	U	L	E	N	N	F	A	C	T	S	U	A	D	O	C
B	E	A	L	U	T	H	I	R	K	B	A	E	T	L	A	S	H
E	R	P	A	S	T	U	W	A	S	U	B	J	E	C	T	M	I
R	E	T	I	T	L	E	F	L	P	A	O	M	R	S	E	O	L
B	A	R	M	R	O	K	C	H	I	P	O	S	T	R	Q	S	D
R	M	S	E	A	R	C	H	I	N	T	K	G	R	A	V	I	R
E	P	A	R	T	S	P	E	T	E	M	C	O	K	T	S	R	E
A	U	T	H	O	R	T	C	H	L	I	B	R	A	R	I	A	N
D	E	S	P	R	I	N	K	A	A	L	W	T	H	I	S	T	S
P	S	I	R	H	T	M	O	O	B	O	O	K	M	A	R	K	O
O	A	M	I	T	F	Q	U	S	E	A	M	E	R	T	Y	O	G
S	I	P	M	S	C	A	T	A	L	O	G	R	I	B	P	T	Y

WORDS TO LOOK FOR:

WORDS APPEAR HORIZONTALLY AND VERTICALLY
NO DIAGONAL OR BACKWARD WORDS

AUTHOR	FINE
BOOK	ILLUSTRATOR
BOOKMARK	LIBRARIAN
CALL NUMBER	LIBRARY CARD
CATALOG	NONFICTION
CHECK OUT	READ
CHILDREN'S	SEARCH
COMPUTER	SPINE LABEL
DUE DATE	SUBJECT
FICTION	TITLE

ANSWER SHEET

Library Terms Word Search Puzzle Answer Key

C						F	I	N	E						
A						I									
L	I	B	R	A	R	Y	C	A	R	D		C			
L						T						O		D	
N	O	N	F	I	C	T	I	O	N			M		U	
U			L		O							P		E	
M			L		N							U		D	C
B			U									T		A	H
E			S					S	U	B	J	E	C	T	I
R		T	I	T	L	E		P		O		R		E	L
			R		C			I		O					D
R		S	E	A	R	C	H	N		K					R
E			T		E			E							E
A	U	T	H	O	R	C	L	I	B	R	A	R	I	A	N
D			R		K					A					S
					O			B	O	O	K	M	A	R	K
					U			E							
			C	A	T	A	L	O	G						

LIBRARY TERMS CROSSWORD PUZZLE

Across:
   2. What you must pay if you don't return your item on time
   3. What you use to check out materials from the library
   6. Factual material
   9. What the book is about
  11. The name of the book
  14. To look for an item
  15. The person who writes the book
  16. A person who works at the library who can help you find what you want
  17. What to put in a book to remember what page you were on
  18. What you look in to find the item you want

Down:
   1. The code that identifies an item in the library
   2. Made-up stories
   4. A tool to help you look up materials in the library
   5. The day the item should be returned to the library
   7. The person who draws the pictures for a book
   8. The department in the library where you will find materials at your reading level
   9. The sticker on the book that matches the call number
  10. Printed item found in the library
  12. What you need to do to take a book home
  13. What you do with a book

ANSWER SHEET

Library Terms Crossword Puzzle

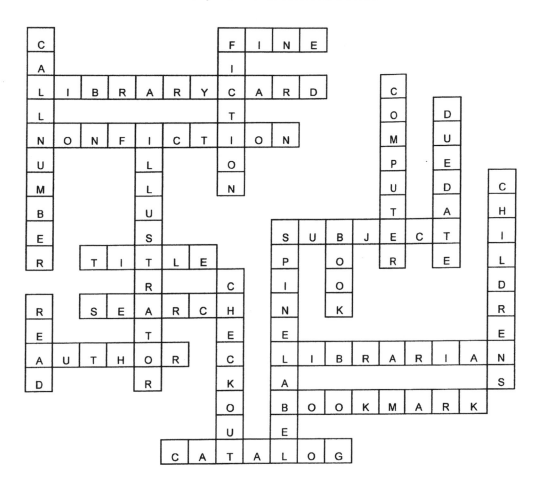

COLLECTION AREAS WORD SEARCH PUZZLE

T	H	N	O	V	E	L	L	O	V	W	D	F	G	U	M	O	P
E	M	S	A	D	A	P	W	A	S	R	K	I	R	U	V	A	R
R	C	B	N	S	S	R	I	R	A	O	I	F	T	X	I	S	A
F	H	U	W	O	Y	O	N	E	K	L	A	G	N	O	D	V	D
P	I	C	T	U	R	E	O	F	O	L	K	L	O	R	E	R	D
S	A	R	P	M	E	V	P	E	L	F	I	B	N	T	O	A	B
A	I	N	G	Y	A	R	O	R	P	I	N	G	F	I	C	Q	N
F	B	O	A	R	D	I	T	E	R	A	S	H	I	D	T	P	O
T	A	B	L	U	E	S	U	N	O	M	A	X	C	D	R	O	M
Y	P	A	P	E	R	B	A	C	K	Y	N	O	T	R	A	T	S
O	T	U	R	V	P	O	K	E	Y	B	R	A	I	L	L	E	S
R	U	D	M	R	E	D	I	V	T	C	R	L	O	S	A	L	O
T	A	I	J	O	R	K	M	A	G	A	Z	I	N	E	M	A	F
U	P	O	E	T	R	Y	A	P	R	E	T	I	N	O	P	T	G
R	S	B	N	I	O	V	Q	T	Y	X	S	M	A	T	Y	L	Y
B	I	O	G	R	A	P	H	Y	E	V	P	C	M	Y	E	S	Y
I	L	O	C	Y	K	S	W	R	T	E	B	U	I	M	P	R	O
J	O	K	L	A	M	E	R	Y	U	G	D	G	W	O	M	V	Q

WORDS APPEAR HORIZONTALLY AND VERTICALLY
NO DIAGONAL OR BACKWARD WORDS

WORDS TO LOOK FOR:

AUDIOBOOK	NONFICTION
BIOGRAPHY	NOVEL
BOARD	PAPERBACK
BRAILLE	PICTURE
CD-ROM	POETRY
DVD	REFERENCE
EASY READER	VIDEO
FOLKLORE	
MAGAZINE	

ANSWER SHEET

Collection Areas Word Search Puzzle

		N	O	V	E	L											
					A										V		
					S			R							I		
					Y			E					N		D	V	D
P	I	C	T	U	R	E		F	O	L	K	L	O	R	E		
					E			E					N		O		
					A			R					F				
	B	O	A	R	D			E					I				
					E			N					C	D	R	O	M
	P	A	P	E	R	B	A	C	K				T				
		U						E		B	R	A	I	L	L	E	
		D											O				
		I					M	A	G	A	Z	I	N	E			
	P	O	E	T	R	Y											
		B															
B	I	O	G	R	A	P	H	Y									
		O															
		K															

COLLECTION AREAS CROSSWORD PUZZLE

Across:
1. A book with chapters
6. A film disc
7. _____book–A book with lots of illustrations
8. A legendary story
9. _____book–A sturdy book for babies
10. Computer software
11. A soft bound book
13. _____book–A book for blind people to read
14. Reading material that is published monthly
15. A book of verses, often in rhyme
16. A book about someone's life

Down:
2. A book for someone who is learning to read
3. A film cassette
4. A book to help with homework that does not leave the library
5. A book with true facts
12. A book on cassette of CD

ANSWER SHEET

Collection Areas Crossword Puzzle

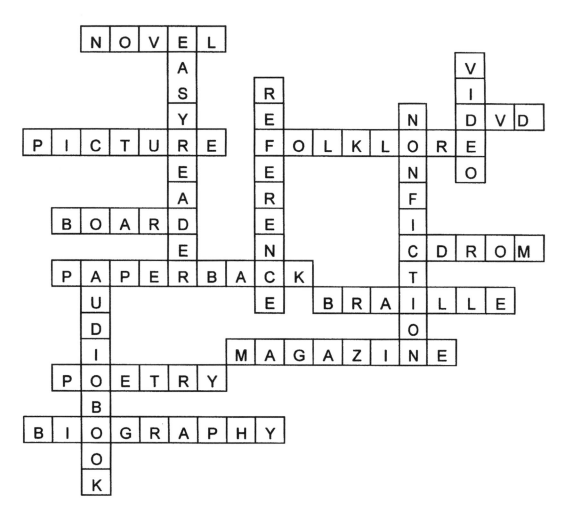

POST-VISIT ACTIVITY SHEET:
KINDERGARTEN AND FIRST GRADE STUDENTS

Today I Went with My Class to Visit _____
                                                    (name of library)

Here is a picture of me at the library:

Here is a picture of my favorite part of my visit to the library:

POST-VISIT ACTIVITY SHEET: GRADES 2–3

Today I went with my class to visit _____
                                    (name of library)
at _____
                          (address)
The Children's Department is located: _____
                                        (location in library)
(Check one): ❏ I received a library card today   ❏ I already had a library card

Every book has a code to help us find it. The code is called a: _____

Books can be checked out for _____ weeks.

We used the computer to look up: _____

One new thing I learned about the library was: _____

_____

The thing I liked best about the visit was: _____

_____

The book I checked out is: _____

Written by: _____

The spine label of this book says: _____

It is due back to the library on: _____

Next time I go to go library, I will look for: _____

Post-Visit Activity Sheet: Grades 4–6

Name: _____   Library card number: _____

The (Name of Library) is located at:

_____
(address)

I learned that I can ask the librarians to help me _____

_____

Some of the materials I can check out are _____

_____

I can use the library computers to _____

_____

My favorite thing to read is _____

_____

In addition to finding books, I can go to the library to _____

_____

The best part about the visit was _____

_____

because _____

_____

Next time I go to the library, I want to _____

_____

Anytown Public Library
Street Address
City, State 00000

THANKS FOR VISITING THE CHILDREN'S DEPARTMENT!

DID YOU KNOW:

☺ We can help you find a book to read for fun

☺ You can put a book on hold if someone else is using it

☺ We can help you find information for homework assignments

☺ You can also find videos, DVDs, audiobooks, and software at the library

☺ You can use our word processors to write papers for school

☺ We have the Internet and online databases

☺ We have special programs for kids your age

☺ You can look us up on our Web site at: www.AnytownLibrary.org

☺ That you can do all these things for FREE at the library!

Anytown Public Library
Street Address
City, State 00000

THANKS FOR VISITING THE CHILDREN'S DEPARTMENT!

DID YOU KNOW:

☺ We can help you find a book to read for fun

☺ You can put a book on hold if someone else is using it

☺ We can help you find information for homework assignments

☺ You can also find videos, DVDs, audiobooks, and software at the library

☺ You can use our word processors to write papers for school

☺ We have the Internet and online databases

☺ We have special programs for kids your age

☺ You can look us up on our Web site at: www.AnytownLibrary.org

☺ That you can do all these things for FREE at the library!

Anytown Public Library		**Anytown Public Library**	
Street Address		Street Address	
City, State 00000		City, State 00000	

CHILDREN'S DEPARTMENT

Phone number:
Fax number:
Web site address:

Collections for young children:

Board books	BD
Picture books	PJ
Easy Readers	E

Collections for children in grades 3–6:

Juvenile chapter books	J
Paperback fiction	JPB
Juvenile nonfiction	J000.000
Juvenile biography	JB
Graphic novels	J Comic
Juvenile reference	JR000.000

Media Collections:

Books on tape	J Cassette
Books on CD	JCD
Computer games	JCD-ROM
Juvenile videos	JVC
Juvenile DVDs	JDVD

We also have:

| Juvenile magazines | JM |
| Parents' collection | PC |

Computer resources:
Online catalog
Internet
Word processing
Games

CHILDREN'S DEPARTMENT

Phone number:
Fax number:
Web site address:

Collections for young children:

Board books	BD
Picture books	PJ
Easy Readers	E

Collections for children in grades 3–6:

Juvenile chapter books	J
Paperback fiction	JPB
Juvenile nonfiction	J000.000
Juvenile biography	JB
Graphic novels	J Comic
Juvenile reference	JR000.000

Media Collections:

Books on tape	J Cassette
Books on CD	JCD
Computer games	JCD-ROM
Juvenile videos	JVC
Juvenile DVDs	JDVD

We also have:

| Juvenile magazines | JM |
| Parents' collection | PC |

Computer resources:
Online catalog
Internet
Word processing
Games

APPENDIX E

Plans, Letters, and Forms: Secondary School Class Visits

Class Visit and Assignment Planning:

Class Visit Day Schedule
Class Visit Day Schedule Short Version
Sample Staff Lists
Timeline for Class Visit Preparation
Library Resources Finder
Library Scavenger Hunt for Teens
Research Materials Worksheet

Letters and Forms:

Teacher Letter
Teacher/Chaperone Evaluation Form
Teen Library Card Application
Teen Services Program Sign-Up Form
Teen Student Evaluation Form
Young Adult Department Bookmark

CLASS VISIT DAY SCHEDULE

9:15–9:25 *The class arrives and the librarian*:

- Welcomes students to library, provides a brief tour
- Addresses the reasons for the orientation
- Divides the class into smaller groups (shown here as A, B, C)

   (Adjust the number of groups and lessons to suit your situation.)

Each individual lesson is assigned a station as:

- Station 1—a computer with the library's online catalog
- Station 2—a computer with databases for research
- Station 3—the Young Adult area

Each lesson is assigned to one librarian who provides the same instruction three times or each librarian stays with his/her group and teaches each lesson once.

	Group A	Group B	Group C
9:25–9:40	Station 1 (online catalog)	Station 2 (YA area)	Station 3 (database)
9:40–9:55	Station 3 (database)	Station 1 (online catalog)	Station 2 (YA area)
9:55–10:10	Station 2 (YA area)	Station 3 (database)	Station 1 (online catalog)

10:10–10:20 *When the lessons are completed, the librarians*:

- Hand out sign-up forms for future programs
- Distribute library cards

The students:

- Complete evaluation forms
- Select materials to check out

The teachers:

- Complete evaluation forms

10:20–10:30 *Librarians*:

- Instruct teens to gather their belongings and materials they selected
- Take teens to circulation desk for check out
- Wrap up with points of interest and remind teens to return

10:30 Students board the bus.

   If there is a second class, it arrives now and the schedule repeats.

CLASS VISIT DAY SCHEDULE SHORT VERSION

(*Note*: This version is designed to fit on a 3" × 5" index card. You can keep this in your pocket during the class visit to check your time.)

9:15–9:25	Greet class, tour, divide into three groups		
	Group A	**Group B**	**Group C**
9:25–9:40	Station 1 (catalog)	Station 2 (YA area)	Station 3 (database)
9:40–9:55	Station 3 (database)	Station 1 (catalog)	Station 2 (YA area)
9:55–10:10	Station 2 (YA area)	Station 3 (database)	Station 1 (catalog)
10:10–10:20	Sign-up forms, evaluations, library cards, select materials		
10:20–10:30	Gather belongings & materials, move to Circ, class leaves. Next class arrives; repeat.		

SAMPLE STAFF LISTS

A secondary school class visit will affect the staffing needs of other departments besides Youth Services. Some of the general factors to be considered are:

- What entrance will the class be using if arriving before the library opens? If the library is already open?
- Will there be more than one class visiting on a given day?
- What time will the first class arrive and will it be before the library opens to the public?
- Will students be allowed to check out books and other materials, including media?
- Will they check out books themselves or will a staff member take care of checking them out?
- Does your library have a computer lab and/or program area that is separate from your department?
- What grade level is the class and what elements will you include in the visit?
- Into how many groups will the class be divided?
- Will there be other programs going on at the time of the class visit?
- Will students be instructed in one or several online databases during the visit?

The following exercises present a variety of factors to help you plan the number of building-wide library staff required for a class visit.

Assumptions for a Sixth Grade Class Visit:

- Two sixth grade classes from an elementary school will visit.
- The purpose of the visit is a transition orientation to Teen Services for their advancement to middle school next year.
- The first class will arrive at 9:15 AM, before the library opens at 10:00 AM.
- The visit will take one hour and 15 minutes.
- The second class will arrive at 10:30 AM, as the first class is leaving.
- The Teen area is on the main floor, with no separate entrance from outside.
- Once they arrive and are escorted to the Teen area, each class of 24 students will be welcomed and divided into three groups, and each group will have at least one parent chaperone, not including the teacher.
- The Teen area on the main level houses the YA book and media collections.
- Three areas will be used for the class visit. The online catalog instruction will take place at two computers adjacent to the Teen area. The database instruction will take place at two other computers adjacent to the Teen area. Students will be seated at tables in the Teen area for the introduction to YA resources and programs. (Note: It is important to locate the three groups sufficiently apart from each other so that one group does not overhear another.)

- Books are checked out at the circulation desk in the lobby and students will check out their own books as they leave the library.

- There will not be any other programs going on at the time of the visit, but other patrons will be able to use the library when it opens at 10 am.

For a Sixth Grade Class Visit, You Will Need at Least:

- **One** custodian or other person responsible for opening the building, turning on lights, etc.

- **One** person at Circulation to check out books and process last minute applications

- **Three** Teen or Youth Services' librarians to lead the three groups (including one who will greet class as they arrive and take them to the Teen area)

- **One** additional librarian arriving before the library opens at 10:00 am to assist other patrons. This librarian can also greet the 10:30 AM class in the lobby if they arrive before the first class has finished.

- **One** optional support staff member to help students find books and troubleshoot if needed.

Assumptions for a Seventh Grade Class Visit:

- One seventh grade middle school class will visit.

- The purposes of the visit are to receive a transition orientation to Teen Services and to begin research on a new assignment.

- The class will arrive at 10:00 am, after the library opens at 9:00 am.

- The visit will take one hour and 15 minutes.

- The class will arrive through the main entrance on the first floor.

- The Teen area is on the upper level of the building.

- There is a computer lab on the upper level which has ten patron computers and is staffed separately. It has been reserved exclusively for the class visit.

- Upon entering, the class of 24 students will be led upstairs to the Teen area and divided into two groups. Each group will have at least one parent chaperone, not including the teacher.

- Two areas will be used for the class visit. Students will be seated at tables in the Teen area for the welcome and introduction to YA resources and programs. The online catalog lesson and database instruction will take place in the computer lab. Students can then do research at the computers or return to the Teen area to take notes for their assigned topics.

- A cart of YA materials including reference books, circulating nonfiction, and media pertaining to their assignment will be available in the Teen area for the class to use.

- Books will be checked out at the circulation desk in the main lobby by the students.

- There will not be any other programs going on at the time of the visit, but other patrons are likely to be using the area since the library is open. Patrons will not be allowed to use the computer lab while the class visit is in session.

For a Seventh Grade Class Visit, You Will Need at Least:

- **One** custodian or other person responsible for opening the building, turning on lights, etc.
- **One** person at Circulation to check out books and process last minute applications
- **One** Teen Services librarian to meet the class in the lobby, bring them to the Teen area, and introduce them to the department and its resources. This librarian will stay in the Teen area to help the students who return here to research their projects.
- **One** librarian or technician to demonstrate the online resources in the computer lab
- **One** more Teen Services librarian to demonstrate the online catalog in the computer lab and stay with the students who remain there to do computer research.
- **One** optional support staff member for the entire visit to help other patrons and troubleshoot if needed.

Assumptions for a High School Class Visit:

- One eleventh grade high school class will visit with their English teacher.
- The class will arrive through the main entrance on the first floor.
- The purpose of the visit is for students to continue researching their term papers on American writers that they started the previous week.
- The visit will take place from 10:00 am to 11:15 am, while the library is open to other patrons.
- Teen patrons use the tables and computers in the Adult Reference area, located on the first floor adjacent to a small YA fiction collection for students, grades 9–12.
- The library has one Teen Services Specialist. Librarians from the Adult and Children's Services departments also work with teen patrons.
- The class of 18 students has been divided into three study clusters grouped by topic (poets, playwrights, and novelists). Each student has notepaper, index cards, pens and other materials, as well as money for the copy machine and computer printer.
- A cart of reference materials and circulating books has been gathered for students to use. They can also search the online catalog and databases for more information.
- Students will be allowed to find materials in other departments, but must bring them back to the tables reserved for them in the Adult Reference area.
- Students will check out books at the circulation desk in the lobby before they leave.

For a High School Class Visit, You Will Need at Least:

- **One** person at Circulation to check out books and process last minute applications

- **One** Teen Services Specialist to gather materials, meet the class and assign the groups to tables that have been reserved for their use. The Teen Services Specialist will discuss the materials gathered on the cart, explain any rules, and help students as needed.

- **One** to two staff members from Adult and Children's Services to assist students who need help finding materials, especially in other areas of the library.

- **One** optional support staff member for the entire visit to help other patrons and troubleshoot if needed.

Assumptions for a High School Class Visit of Students with Special Needs:

- One high school class comprised of ten students with learning disabilities from grades 9 to 12, one teacher and two teacher assistants will visit.

- The class will arrive through the main entrance on the first floor.

- The purposes of the visit are for the students to find out what materials and services are available to them in the library and to check out books on their assigned topics that are appropriate to their levels of learning.

- The visit will take place from 10:30 am to 11:30 am, while the library is open to other patrons.

- Teen patrons use the tables and computers in the Adult Reference area, located on the first floor adjacent to a small YA fiction collection for students, grades 9–12.

- The library has one Teen Services Specialist. Librarians from the Adult and Children's Services departments also work with teen patrons.

- The Teen Services Specialist will greet the class in the lobby and lead them to tables in Adult Reference which have been reserved for their use. After a brief a welcome to the library, the Teen Services Specialist will show the students some materials (gathered on a cart) that are relevant to their research topics and appropriate to their reading abilities.

- The class will be divided into smaller groups based upon the students' abilities, their research topics, and the staff available. Each librarian will stay with his/her assigned group throughout the visit.

- Librarians will show the students in their groups how to search for information using the online catalog on computers located near their tables.

- Students may select books from the cart to check out. Students who want to look for materials in other areas will be accompanied by a library staff member and/or a teacher.

- Students will meet back at the tables and move as a group to the circulation desk in the lobby to check out their books before exiting the building.

Note: It is imperative that the teacher(s) come to the library to meet with the library staff ahead of time to prepare for an entire class of students with special needs. The concerns that need to be considered are:

- The academic abilities of the students, including the range of reading levels (appropriate books can be gathered in advance)

- The attention spans of the students

- Their familiarity with the library and how to behave there

- Gathering fiction and nonfiction books from various areas around the library that the students would be able to read and understand

- Any additional information the teacher(s) can provide to help the librarians prepare, such as whether or not computers with assistive technology would be needed

For a High School Class Visit of Students with Special Needs You Will Need at Least:

- **One** person at Circulation to check out books and process last minute applications

- **One** Teen Services Specialist to meet with the teachers ahead of time, organize the visit, and provide the opening lesson.

- **Two** to three staff members from Adult and Children's Services to demonstrate the online catalog, and to help the students choose books on different floors

These lists are bare bones requirements for several class visit scenarios and do not consider staff needed to operate the rest of the library.

TIMELINE FOR CLASS VISIT PREPARATION

While the school liaison is scheduling the secondary school visits:

- Prepare templates for letters to teachers
- Prepare teacher and student evaluation forms
- Prepare any activity sheets you will use with students during the visit and/or to give teachers to use with the class after they return to school
- Develop any brochures, book lists, or other materials you want to give to teachers
- Obtain envelopes for teacher letters, folders for teacher packets, and library card applications
- Determine exactly what you will cover during the visit, how it will be done, and who will do it
- Make a schedule of what will happen on the day of the visit, indicating the time each part should occur
- Design any materials to use during the visit and order bookmarks to give to students

When you receive the schedule from your school liaison:

- Verify the teachers' names and the number of students in each class on the schedule
- Check the dates against your calendar to make sure they are workable
- Inform other departments of the class visit schedule and make sure there are no conflicts
- Notify the school liaison of any conflicts ASAP and reschedule dates if needed
- Meet with staff scheduled to do visits; modify routines as needed; discuss lessons and schedule prep time
- Meet with scheduled staff again to finalize lessons and practice online searches
- Reserve the computer lab for class visit dates (if applicable)

Three to four weeks prior to each visit:

- Print all materials needed including letters, brochures and library card applications
- Assemble and mail pre-visit packets to teachers

One week prior to each visit:

- Check for the return of library card applications; call the teacher if needed
- Prepare new library cards; call teacher or parents if there are problems
- Prepare materials and count out bookmarks to give class
- Assemble post-visit materials for teacher packet

Two days prior to each visit:

- Call the teacher to remind him/her about the upcoming visit
- Make sure the library cards are done and in your department

One day prior to each visit:

- Gather and set aside all needed materials, including YA program sign-up and volunteer forms, pencils, evaluations, teachers' packets, and bookmarks
- Remind the custodian, Circulation staff, and other staff of the next day's visit
- Prepare a cart of YA resources, including books and media for lessons and discussion
- Make sure all computers are working and test online searches

The day of each visit:

- Arrive at least 15 minutes before the class is due
- Set up areas and materials
- Turn on and test computers
- Check to make sure a Circulation clerk and other staff outside of your department who are involved with the class visit have arrived
- Station one person at the designated entrance to greet the class
- If you are not doing the teacher and student evaluations during the visit, make sure that you give each teacher the evaluations in a stamped, self-addressed envelope and ask them to return it to you ASAP.
- **CONDUCT THE CLASS VISIT!**

Immediately after each visit:

- Return areas to normal and put away materials
- Thank staff verbally for their efforts, especially those outside your department

After all class visits are completed:

- Read evaluations and compile data
- Meet with department members to discuss what worked and what needs to be changed
- Thank staff in other departments publicly, perhaps with an all staff email, for their cooperation and assistance with the visits
- Report class visit statistics and teacher evaluation summary to library director
- Contact the school liaison to share feedback and discuss what worked and what needs to be changed
- Resume your "normal" schedule!

[your library header here]

LIBRARY RESOURCES FINDER

Student's Name: _____ Date: _____

Teacher: _____ Grade: _____

Topic: _____

Use the skills learned during your library visit to find the following resources on this topic: _____

Reference book:

 Title: _____

 Call #: _____

Circulating book:

 Title: _____

 Call #: _____

Magazine article:

 Magazine title: _____

 Article title: _____

 Date of article: _____

 Page numbers: _____

Media:

 Type of media: _____

 Title: _____

 Call #: _____

Database or Internet source:

 Title of database or Web site: _____

 Web site address: _____

[your library header here]

LIBRARY SCAVENGER HUNT FOR TEENS

Try this scavenger hunt to test your comprehension of the library skills demonstrated during your recent class visit. The goal is for you to explore resources so you can determine the best ones to use for your own research assignments.

You may write your answers on the back of this sheet or on a separate piece of paper. Begin your search in the Teen area.

1. Record the names of two library staff members and their job titles.

2. What does it cost for each page you want to print or photocopy at Anytown Public Library?

3. List the titles of two magazines in the library that interest you and where they are located.

4. Find a Teen biography about someone of interest to you and record the book's title, author, and call number.

5. Find a Teen fiction book by an author whose last name begins with the same letter of the alphabet as your last name. Record the title, author, and call number.

6. Find a Teen book that is available on tape or CD and record the title, author, and call number.

7. Find a Teen music CD and record the title, artist, and call number.

8. In the library's online catalog, look up a favorite author and record the number of books that the library owns by that author.

9. Pick a subject of interest to you and list two Teen reference books on that subject. Record the titles and call numbers.

10. Introduce yourself to one of the Teen or Children's librarians and ask for an interesting fact about them for you to record.

[your library header here]

RESEARCH MATERIALS WORKSHEET

Use this sheet to record the resources you consult during your class visit to the library. Use a separate sheet for each resource.

Source _____

Source # _____

Student: _____ Teacher: _____

Assignment: _____

Project Title: _____

Other students working on this project: _____

_____

Today's Date: _____ Project Due Date: _____

Resource used: ❏ Book ❏ Periodical ❏ Internet ❏ CD-ROM

 ❏ Other (explain) _____

Name of Book, Periodical, or Database: _____

_____

Publisher and Date: _____

Title of Chapter or Article: _____

Author: _____

Page(s): _____

Brief Summary of Information: _____

_____

_____

_____

_____

Where/How I will Use this Information: _____

_____

_____

_____

_____

_____

Use this Information with Source(s) # _____

TEACHER LETTER

[your library header here]

Teacher
Middle or High School
Street
Anytown, State, 00000

[Today's Date]

Dear Teacher,

We are pleased to welcome you and your sixth grade students to the Anytown Public Library on day of the week, month, date, year. A school bus will pick up your class at the school and bring you to the Anytown Public Library. Someone from the staff will be waiting to greet you and your students at the library's parking lot entrance at 9:15 A.M. and escort you into the library. The bus will pick up your class at the conclusion of the class visit at 10:30 A.M. and return you to school.

We would like your class to have an enjoyable and productive visit. In order to facilitate this, we request that you assist us by doing the following:

1. Arrange to have three chaperones, including yourself, accompany the class, since the students will be divided into three groups during the visit.
2. All chaperones should remain with their assigned group for the duration of the visit and assist their group as necessary.
3. Notify us in advance of any unusual circumstances or if any of your students require special assistance.

Since the students will be checking out books as part of their visit, it is important that each student bring a valid library card with them, if they have one. For those who do not, we are enclosing library card applications. You may make copies if needed. Please assist your students in filling these out by checking the following:

1. The students must **print** legibly all information on the application.
2. Students must **sign** the application in the space provided.
3. Any student who has lost his/her library card should fill out an application.

Please distribute the library card applications to your students immediately and return them to the library batched together with your name and the school's name clearly written on the outside of the envelope along with the scheduled date of your visit. We prefer that you bring them in to our Circulation Department in person, to assure that the forms arrive safely. If that is not possible, please send them via the mail. We must receive the applications at least one week before the class visit date in order to process them in time.

Thank you in advance for your cooperation. Please call us if you have any questions or special requirements. We look for to meeting you and you students!

Sincerely,
Your Name, Young Adult Librarian

Note: Substitute your information throughout the letter as needed. You may want to include additional information in your letter, such as:

- Any other information that is required on the library card application
- Instructions for permission forms for the class trip
- What to do if a child has fines on his/her library card
- What to do if a child is from out of town and is not able to obtain a card from your library
- Your library's policy for overdue books
- Information about the Teacher Loan Card
- Information about the evaluation form that you will ask teachers to complete on class visit day
- The name of the library building where the visit will occur and the address if your public library has more than one branch.
- Asking the teacher to inform you of any students with special needs and of any non–English speaking students so accommodations can be arranged

TEACHER/CHAPERONE EVALUATION FORM

(Note: Customize as needed to reflect the elements included in your presentation. The form should take up one side of a letter-size sheet of paper.)

[your library header here]

School: _____   Date: _____

Your name: _____

This form is filled out by a (check one):
❑ Teacher   ❑ Media Specialist   ❑ Parent Chaperone   ❑ Other

1. Did you find this visit helpful to your students?
❑ Yes, very helpful   ❑ Somewhat helpful   ❑ Not helpful

2. Was the overall presentation well organized?
❑ Yes, very organized   ❑ Somewhat organized   ❑ Not organized

3. Was the library staff knowledgeable?
❑ Yes, very knowledgeable   ❑ Somewhat knowledgeable   ❑ Not knowledgeable

4. Rank the lessons in order of importance
   (1= most important, 4= least important).
___ Online catalog instruction   ___ Database lesson
___ Young Adult resources and programs   ___ Materials selection

5. About how often to you visit Anytown Public Library? _____

6. Do you have an Anytown Public Library teacher loan card?
❑ Yes   ❑ No

7. Would you like us to add or cut anything from the class visit?
_____

8. Please consider buying these materials: _____
9. Please consider offering a program on: _____
10. Other comments: _____
_____
_____

ANYTOWN PUBLIC LIBRARY
TEEN LIBRARY CARD APPLICATION

PLEASE PRINT LEGIBLY   Date _____

Last Name _____ First Name _____ Initial _____

Home Address: Street _____

City _____ State _____ Zip Code _____

Home Phone Number _____ Cell Phone (optional) _____

Date of Birth: Month/Date/Year _____

Email address (If you want to receive overdue/hold notices via email) _____

I agree to obey the rules of Anytown Public Library and to be responsible for all charges incurred for any overdue, lost or damaged materials. In the event my card is lost or stolen, I understand that I am responsible for charges on and until the date I notify the library of the loss or theft of my card.

Signature of Applicant (Teen) _____

ANYTOWN PUBLIC LIBRARY
TEEN OR YOUTH SERVICES DEPARTMENT
PHONE NUMBER

ANYTOWN PUBLIC LIBRARY
TEEN LIBRARY CARD APPLICATION

PLEASE PRINT LEGIBLY   Date _____

Last Name _____ First Name _____ Initial _____

Home Address: Street _____

City _____ State _____ Zip Code _____

Home Phone Number _____ Cell Phone (optional) _____

Date of Birth: Month/Date/Year _____

Email address (If you want to receive overdue/hold notices via email) _____

I agree to obey the rules of Anytown Public Library and to be responsible for all charges incurred for any overdue, lost or damaged materials. In the event my card is lost or stolen, I understand that I am responsible for charges on and until the date I notify the library of the loss or theft of my card.

Signature of Applicant (Teen) _____

ANYTOWN PUBLIC LIBRARY
TEEN OR YOUTH SERVICES DEPARTMENT
PHONE NUMBER

[your library header here]

TEEN SERVICES PROGRAM SIGN-UP FORM

Date _____   School _____

Last Name _____   First Name _____

Street address _____

City _____   State _____   Zip Code _____

Phone _____

I am interested in receiving information about:

❑ Book discussion groups

❑ Volunteer programs

Teen Student Evaluation Form

Teacher: _____ School: _____ Date: _____

Please help us to know what we can do to make your visit better by checking the appropriate box for each question:

1. The overall presentation was:

❑ Useful ❑ Somewhat useful ❑ Not useful

2. I already knew the information about the:

Catalog ❑ Most of it ❑ Some ❑ None
Database(s) ❑ Most of it ❑ Some ❑ None
YA area ❑ Most of it ❑ Some ❑ None

3. The information in the lessons will be:

❑ Very valuable for assignments ❑ Somewhat valuable for assignments

4. I use the public library:

❑ All the time ❑ Often ❑ Now and then ❑ Never

5. I would like you to buy: _____

6. I would like you to offer: _____

7. Comments: _____

ANYTOWN PUBLIC LIBRARY
Street Address
City, State, Zip

YOUNG ADULT DEPARTMENT
PHONE #
WEB SITE
DEPARTMENT LINK NAME

Homework Desk Hours:

Monday	AM–PM
Tuesday	AM–PM
Wednesday	AM–PM
Thursday	AM–PM
Friday	AM–PM
Saturday	AM–PM

Information for assignments:

Young Adult Reference
Young Adult Nonfiction
Young Adult Fiction
Young Adult Media

Online Databases:

Periodical search databases
Subscription databases

Technology for assignments:

    60 minute sessions
    $ .15/page to print
    $1.00 for discs

Wireless Internet access

Computer lab available with:

    Microsoft Word
    Excel
    PowerPoint
    Publisher

Visit us 24/7 at
www.Anytownlibrary.org

ANYTOWN PUBLIC LIBRARY
Street Address
City, State, Zip

YOUNG ADULT DEPARTMENT
PHONE #
WEB SITE
DEPARTMENT LINK NAME

Homework Desk Hours:

Monday	AM–PM
Tuesday	AM–PM
Wednesday	AM–PM
Thursday	AM–PM
Friday	AM–PM
Saturday	AM–PM

Information for assignments:

Young Adult Reference
Young Adult Nonfiction
Young Adult Fiction
Young Adult Media

Online Databases:

Periodical search databases
Subscription databases

Technology for assignments:

    60 minute sessions
    $ .15/page to print
    $1.00 for discs

Wireless Internet access

Computer lab available with:

    Microsoft Word
    Excel
    PowerPoint
    Publisher

Visit us 24/7 at
www.Anytownlibrary.org

Come see what's new @

ANYTOWN PUBLIC LIBRARY
YOUNG ADULT DEPARTMENT

TEEN Fiction
(Highlight new fiction titles)

Teen Title	by John Smith
Teen Title	by John Smith
Teen Title	by John Smith
Teen Title	by John Smith
Teen Title	by John Smith
Teen Title	by John Smith
Teen Title	by John Smith
Teen Title	by John Smith

Teen Media

Try out our new Listening Station!

Teen Music CD	by Artist
Teen Music CD	by Artist
Teen Music CD	by Artist
Teen Music CD	by Artist
Teen DVD	Shelf location
Teen DVD	Shelf location
Teen DVD	Shelf location
Teen CD-ROM	Shelf location
Teen CD-ROM	Shelf location

Special Teen Collections
(Highlight titles)

Teen Biography	Shelf location
Teen Biography	Shelf location
Teen Magazine	Shelf location
Teen Magazine	Shelf location
Graphic Novel	Shelf location
Graphic Novel	Shelf location

Visit us 24/7 at
www.Anytownlibrary.org

Come see what's new @

ANYTOWN PUBLIC LIBRARY
YOUNG ADULT DEPARTMENT

TEEN Fiction
(Highlight new fiction titles)

Teen Title	by John Smith
Teen Title	by John Smith
Teen Title	by John Smith
Teen Title	by John Smith
Teen Title	by John Smith
Teen Title	by John Smith
Teen Title	by John Smith
Teen Title	by John Smith

Teen Media

Try out our new Listening Station!

Teen Music CD	by Artist
Teen Music CD	by Artist
Teen Music CD	by Artist
Teen Music CD	by Artist
Teen DVD	Shelf location
Teen DVD	Shelf location
Teen DVD	Shelf location
Teen CD-ROM	Shelf location
Teen CD-ROM	Shelf location

Special Teen Collections
(Highlight titles)

Teen Biography	Shelf location
Teen Biography	Shelf location
Teen Magazine	Shelf location
Teen Magazine	Shelf location
Graphic Novel	Shelf location
Graphic Novel	Shelf location

Visit us 24/7 at
www.Anytownlibrary.org

Index

Numbers in **boldface** refer to forms and templates.

171

When The
TRUTH
Lies